D0856802

KLIMT

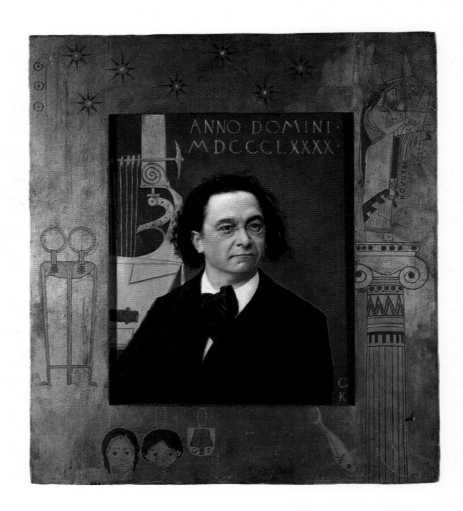

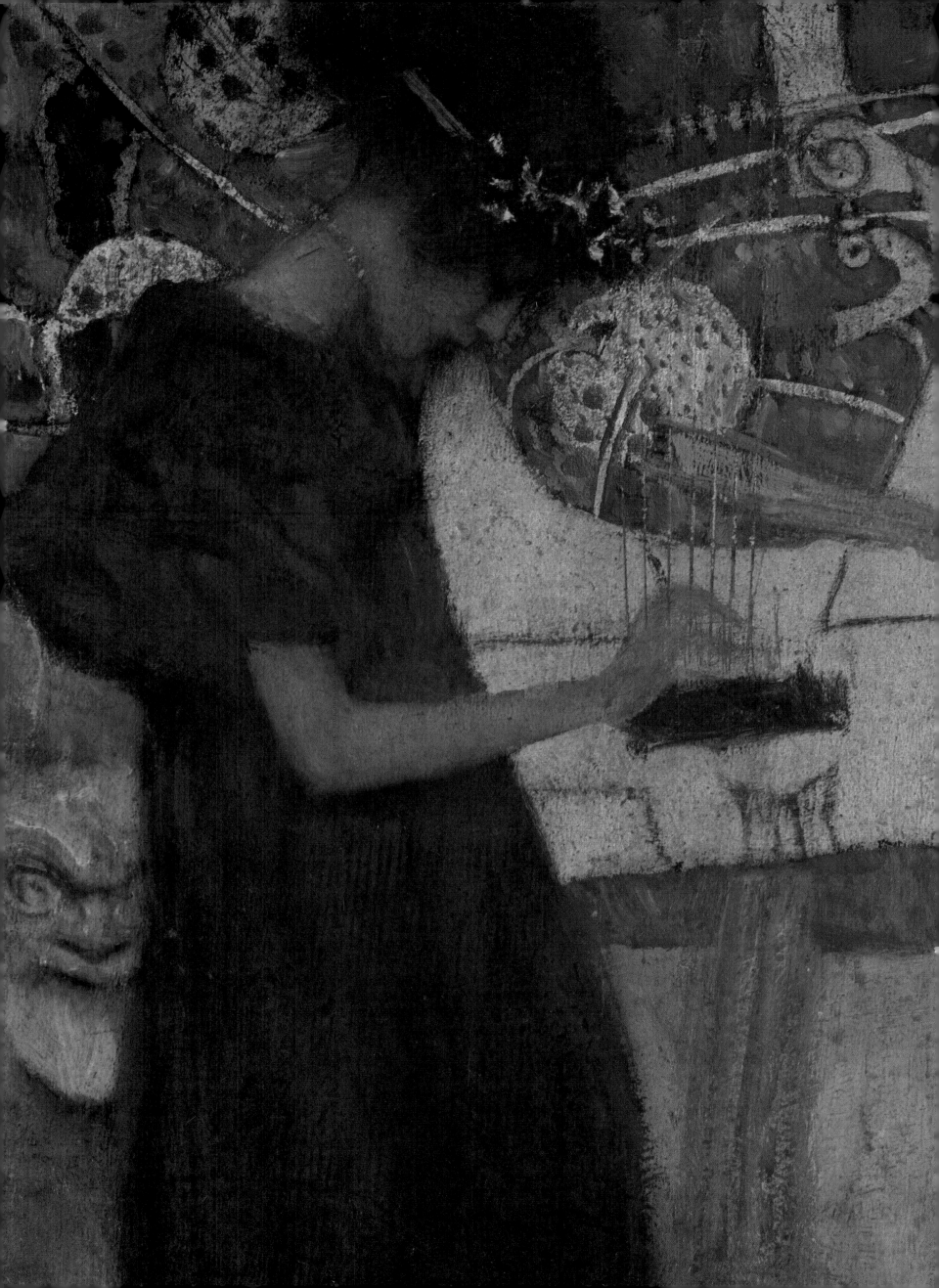

KLIMT

Maria Costantino

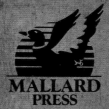

MALLARD PRESS

Copyright © 1990 by Brompton Books
Corporation

First published in the United States of America in
1990
by The Mallard Press
Mallard Press and its accompanying design and
logo are trademarks of BDD Promotional Book
Company, Inc.

ISBN 0-792-45327-1

Printed in Italy

For Keith and Keith, without whom
this book would never have been.

Page 1: *Portrait of the Pianist and Piano
Teacher Joseph Pembauer*, 1890

Page 2-3: *Music I*, 1895

Contents and List of Plates

Introduction	6	Cottage Garden with Sunflowers	68
		The Sunflower	69
Fable	22	Portrait of Adèle Bloch-Bauer I	71
Idyll	23	Danae	73
Auditorium in the Old Burgtheater	25	Hope II	74
Portrait of the Pianist and Piano Teacher Joseph Pembauer	27	Judith II (Salome)	75
		Schloss Kammer on the Attersee	76
Ancient Greek I and II, Ancient Egyptian I and II	28	Schloss Kammer on the Attersee III	77
		The Kiss	79
Portrait of a Lady (Frau Heymann?)	30	Lady with a Feather Hat	80
Love	31	Lady with a Hat and Feather Boa	81
Music I	32	The Park	83
Tragedy	35	Portrait of Adèle Bloch-Bauer II	85
Portrait of Sonja Knips	37	Avenue in the Park of the Schloss Kammer	87
Pallas Athene	39	Portrait of Mäda Primavesi	89
Medicine	40	Death and Life	91
Nuda Veritas	41	The Virgin	93
Schubert at the Piano	42	Church at Cassone	94
Portrait of Serena Lederer	43	Portrait of Elisabeth Bachofen-Echt	95
Hygieia (detail for Medicine)	45	Unterach on the Attersee	97
Island in the Attersee	46	The Friends	98
Goldfish	47	Portrait of Friederike Maria Beer	99
Portrait of Emilie Flöge	48	The Dancer	101
Beech Wood I	49	The Bride	103
Hope I	50	Baby	105
Water Snakes (Friends I)	51	Adam and Eve	106
Judith I	53	Portrait of Johanna Staude	107
Beethoven Frieze	54	Portrait of a Lady	108
Stoclet Frieze	59	Portrait of a Lady, Facing	109
The Three Ages of Woman	63		
Portrait of Margaret Stonborough-Wittgenstein	65	Bibliography	110
		Index	110
Portrait of Fritza Riedler	67	Acknowledgments	112

Introduction

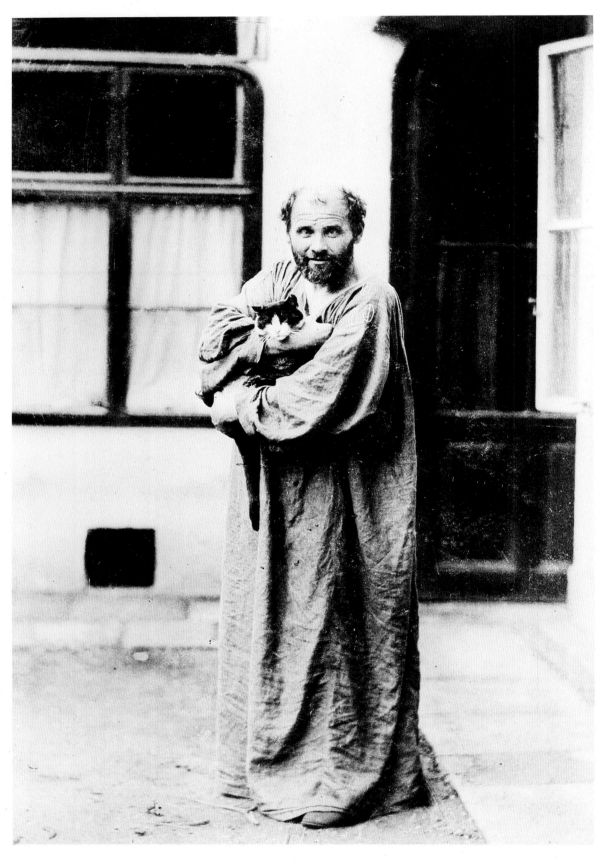

During the period spanning the turn of the century, Vienna was one of the most important cities in the world. By 1900 it was the fourth largest city in Europe with a population of more than two million and, at the center of Austria-Hungary, was the heart of a major European power. In addition, Vienna had gained itself the reputation for not taking the world too seriously and was envied for the quality and diversity of its culture.

Whenever we speak of 'Vienna around 1900' it is the visual arts that first spring to mind. The fin-de-siècle spirit coincided in Vienna with the 'Secession' in March 1897 of nineteen painters and architects led by Gustav Klimt, who was undeniably the most important Austrian painter of these years. Klimt was born in 1862 in Baumgarten, a rural suburb of Vienna, the second of seven children. His parents had come from humble origins: his father,

Ernst Klimt, a goldsmith from Litomerice in Bohemia, had built up a modest trade, while his Viennese mother Anna had once dreamed of a career as a theater singer.

Artistic training in Vienna in the last decades of the nineteenth century was centered in two main institutions, the Academy of Fine Arts (Akademie der bildenden Künste) and the exhibiting society of Künstlerhausgenossenschaft, to which almost all the established artists belonged.

6

The Künstlerhaus was a private organization which owned Vienna's only exhibition building, and as such was able to exert an enormous influence on public taste and government policies on art through their annual exhibitions. Like the Academy, the Künstlerhaus was predominately conservative in its outlook and the 1880s was to be known in retrospect as the 'Makart decade' after the sometime president of the Künstlerhaus, Hans Makart.

There was, however, a rival to the Academy in the form of the Austrian Museum for Art and Industry which had founded its own School of Applied Arts (Künstgewerbeschule), modeled on the Schools of Art at South Kensington in London, later to become the Royal College of Art.

It was to the Kunstgewerbeschule that Klimt went in 1876 to study after receiving a scholarship. He was to remain there for seven years. Later, his brothers Ernst and Georg also attended the school. For two years Klimt followed courses in anatomy, history, technical and specialized drawing under his professors Rieser, Minnegerode and Hrachowisa. Tuition in painting was given by Professor Ferdinard Laufberger, an important figure in Klimt's early artistic career as it was he who first allowed Gustav, his brother Ernst and a fellow student Franz Matsch (1861-1942) to carry out the 'sgraffito' in the courtyards of the Kunsthistorisches Museum in Vienna in 1879.

In the same year the three students also took part in the preparations for Hans Makart's great masked parade around the Ringstrasse in celebration of the Imperial Silver Wedding. Makart himself headed the pageant on horseback, clad in a Renaissance-style red costume. Although now recognized as a master in the field of portraiture, Makart is best remembered for his gigantic compositions depicting Viennese society belles in thirty disguised Renaissance pastiches. It was Makart's personal taste and lifestyle as president of the Künstlerhaus which dominated Viennese society: there is even a 'Makart bouquet' named after his liking for elaborate vases filled with peacock feathers, sheaves of corn, palm leaves and grasses. Undoubtedly a master of his age, Makart was the only painter of his era in Austria to be acknowledged outside his own country and after his death in 1884 his influence continued. Gustav Klimt was regarded as Makart's 'heir' and carried out commissions based on Makart's designs.

In 1880 the Klimt brothers and Franz Matsch between them painted four ceiling panels for the Palais Sturany, a Viennese town house, and following a recommendation from Professor Laufberger, the three were introduced to the theatrical architects Fellner and Helmer, for whom they produced a ceiling panel for the Kur-

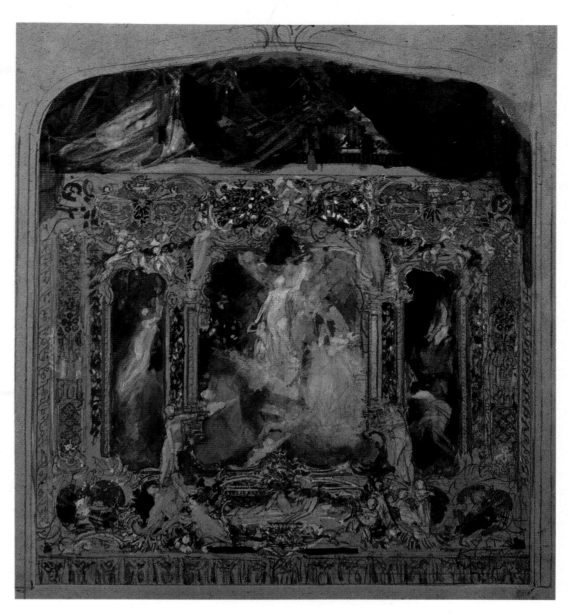

haus (the municipal theater) in Karlsbad (now Karlovy Vary).

Following Laufberger's death in 1881, Gustav and Ernst Klimt and Franz Matsch continued their studies in painting under Professor Julius Viktor Berger. These studies, however, did not stop Klimt from receiving further commissions. In 1881 he was asked by the publisher Martin Gerlach to supply designs for a publication of *Allegories and Emblems,* a collection of patterns and designs in the manner of historical paintings, and for which Klimt drew *The Four Seasons.* With his brother and Matsch, Klimt was also working on decorative paintings for the Romanian royal palace at Pelesch, situated in the forest near Sinaia and for decorative works for Reichenberg (Liberec). Increasingly their style was in keeping with the ideals of Makart and also revealed the influence of the old masters. For the ancestral portraits based on engravings for the Romanian royal commissions, Klimt was copying Titian and the designs for *Allegories and Emblems* reveal the influence of the renaissance, a period much favored by Makart.

By 1883 the Klimt brothers and Matsch had established their own studio in Vienna. In great demand for decorative art, in 1885 the studio was commissioned

Left: Klimt and his cat in the garden of his studio in the Josefstaderstrasse.

Above: The 1886 design for the Karlsbad Theater curtain, based on a design by Hans Makart.

to paint murals for the Hermes Villa in Lainz, near Vienna, built by Karl von Hasenauer. In the same year the studio also produced paintings for the Bucharest Municipal Theater and the Fiume Municipal Theater. Before the Fiume paintings were installed, they were exhibited in Vienna where they were well received by the general public. The real breakthrough for the studio came in 1886 when the young artists were commissioned to ornament the Karlsbad Theater. Gustav painted two ceiling panels and the three painters jointly produced the theater curtain which was based on a design by Makart. But the zenith of Klimt's career as a historical painter was to commission for the ceiling and spandrel paintings for the two staircases of the Burgtheater, a program of works depicting the history of the theater. On the right-hand staircase Klimt painted the *Chariot of Thespis, Shakespeare's Theater* and the *Altar of Dionysus;* on the left-hand staircase: the *Theater in Taormina* and the *Altar of Apollo.* When the paintings were completed two years later, the Gold Cross of merit, the highest artistic honor, was

7

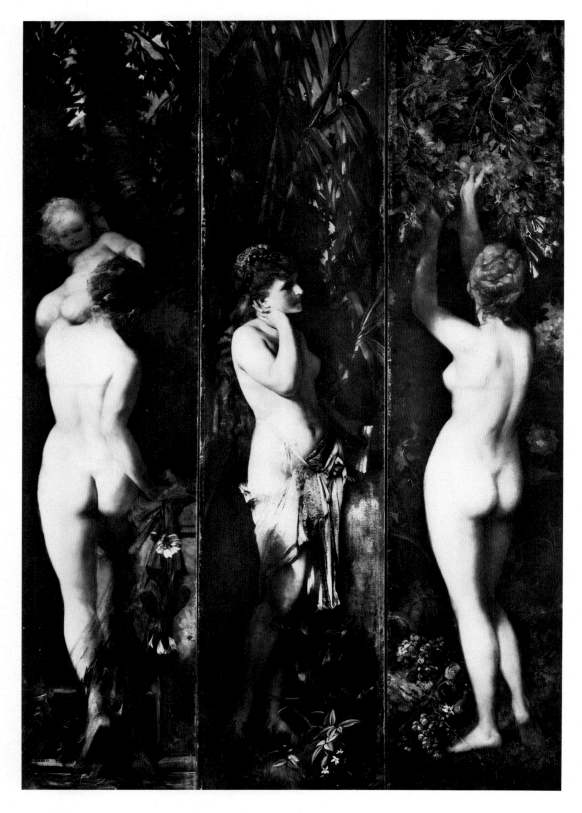

cently been built by Heinrich von Furstel would have a central panel on the theme of the *Triumph of Light over Darkness* plus one of the four side panels, *Theology*, painted by Matsch. The remaining three side panels on the subject of *Philosophy, Medicine* and *Jurisprudence* would be the work of Gustav Klimt. Ernst Klimt, often considered to be the binding force betwen his brother and Matsch had died the previous year. Despite Ernst's death the studio retained the commission.

Where the professors of the University had expected portraits of the great philosophers and men of science, Klimt produced allegories in a highly personal and obscure manner, using many female nudes. These hugh canvasses, regrettably destroyed by fire during the last days of World War II, had such a hostile reception that Klimt eventually bought back the commission in 1905.

What was it that caused Klimt to change so radically his style and approach to painting and what was it about these paintings that so outraged his patrons and the public? It may well have been partly due to the change in Klimt's private life that brought about his new vision full of color and subtleties. In 1893 he had been passed over by the Emperor for the post of Professor of Historical Painting at the Viennese Academy. Furthermore, through the marriage of his brother Ernst to Helen Flöge, one of three daughters of a wealthy family who collectively ran a famous Viennese fashion house, Gustav gained entry into the cultural bourgeoie circles of Viennese society. His sister-in-law Emilie Flöge became a much-loved and often painted friend. Through further contracts provided by his friend and colleague, the painter Carl Moll (whose step-daughter Alma married Gustav Mahler), Klimt was introduced to the Viennese beauties such as Adèle Bloch-Bauer and Margaret Wittgenstein, whose families had not only acquired wealth but a more progressive taste in art. An important event preceding the emergence of the three paintings – *Philosophy* (1900), *Medicine* (1901), and *Jurisprudence* (1903) – was the foundation in 1897 of the Vienna Secession.

The Vienna Secession, led by Klimt, was founded by some of the younger members of the Genossenschaft Bildender Künstler (The association of Visual Artists) as an act of defiance against the teachings of their elders, and like its Munich counterpart, the Vienna Secession wanted to give artists the opportunity of showing their work in public. The existing and highly conservative exhibiting organization, the Genossenschaft, which included in its membership nearly all the established artists in Vienna including Klimt, had the only exhibition space in the city. The Secessionists who

awarded to Klimt by the Emperor Franz Josef. Klimt was now truly Makart's heir, a respected and favored professional painter of historical scenes that satisfied institutional tastes. But this was to be the last work with which Gustav Klimt was accepted in court. Increasingly decorative symbolism was playing a key role in his art and although the studio of Gustav, Ernst and Matsch continued to work together on public commissions, the three artists were developing noticably away from each other. While Matsch remained stylistically bound to the conservative style of decoration, Gustav was turning away from the academic conception of picures by introducing soft-focus impressionistic techniques and the application of decorative materials such as gold and silver leaf in an approach related to Symbolism and Art Nouveau.

Klimt's next commission made clear his stylistic change. The assignment was to complete another Makart legacy to the studio, the influential decorations for the staircase of the Kunsthistorisches Museum in Vienna. Of the 40 spandrels and intercolumnar pictures, Gustav's eleven paintings have as their subject the development of art from ancient Egypt to the cinquecento, with the figures represented in a strict frontality against a ground of gold. In this project, we see the first appearance also of Klimt's 'femme fatale.'

Despite the change in Gustav's approach, the studio work was received favorably and led to the Arts Commission of the Ministry of education awarding the studio the commission to decorate the ceiling of the Great Hall of the University in 1893. The Great Hall which had re-

8

considered the exhibitions at the Künstlerhaus both pretentious and overstocked – the writer Hermann Bahr went as far as to call it a 'bazaar' – sought to educate and inform the Viennese public whom they considered insular and ignorant. The Secession therefore planned to show not only work by Viennese artists but works by their contemporaries abroad. The Viennese on the whole were largely ignorant of artistic developments in France, England and the low countries: few Viennese had even heard of Manet, Gauguin or van Gogh.

After a year of intensive preparations, the first exhibition of the Secession opened at the premises of the Vienna Horticultural Society on 26th March 1898; Klimt designed the exhibition poster depicting Theseus slaying the Minotaur. This poster was objected to by the censors on the grounds of 'immorality'; although there was a long tradition of nudes in paintings and sculptures, never had a nude figure been used for advertising purposes. In order to satisfy the censor, Klimt added the device of a tree to the design, thus obscuring Theseus's offending genitalia. The poster also employed an elaborate symbolism: the upper portion where Theseus delivered the final death blow to the minotaur was designed to symbolize the battle between the Secession and the official Academy, while Athene, long recognized as the symbol of the protector of artist groups, looks on.

In addition to work by Austrian members, on show were exhibits by Arnold Böcklin, Auguste Rodin, Giuseppe Segantini, Max Klinger, Eugène Carriere, James McNeill Whistler, Franz von Stuck and Alphonse Mucha. Pierre Puvis de Chavannes showed the cartoons for the Pantheon in Paris, the *St Genevieve Triptych*; Walter Crane contributed watercolors, stained glass and wallpaper designs while Fernand Khnopff showed a remarkable series of nineteen paintings. Khnopff (1858-1921) had been seen as one

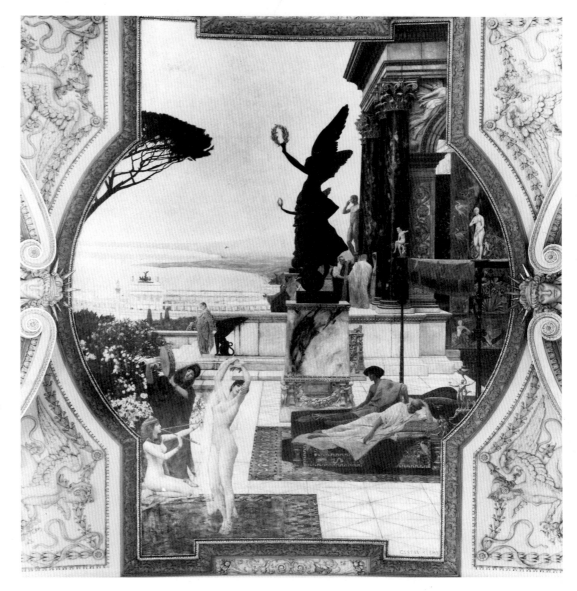

of the most important single influences on the early work of the Secessionists as a whole and of Klimt in particular. He created mysterious works made all the more disturbing by their use of ostensible 'realism' and by the fact that the female types he used in his works are based on the image of his sister Marguerite, whose beauty obsessed him. One painting by Khnopff shown at the first exhibition *Stiff Water* (1895), can be singled out as an example which relates to the style of Klimt's early landscapes.

The success of the first Secession ex-

Left: Makart's academic allegories of the senses *Sight, Hearing* and *Smell*.

Above and below: The *Theater in Taormina* (1886-88) and the *Chariot of Theopis* (1888) from the stairs of the Burgtheater.

hibition surprised even its organizers: the show had 50,000 visitors, thus proving that not all modernism was anathema to the Viennese. With the proceeds of the exhibition, the organization made plans for a building of its own, designed by Josef Maria Olbrich and nick-named the 'Krauthappel' (cabbage-head). The con-

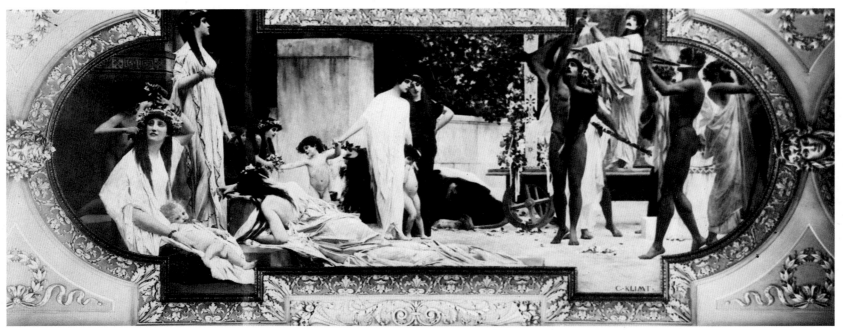

9

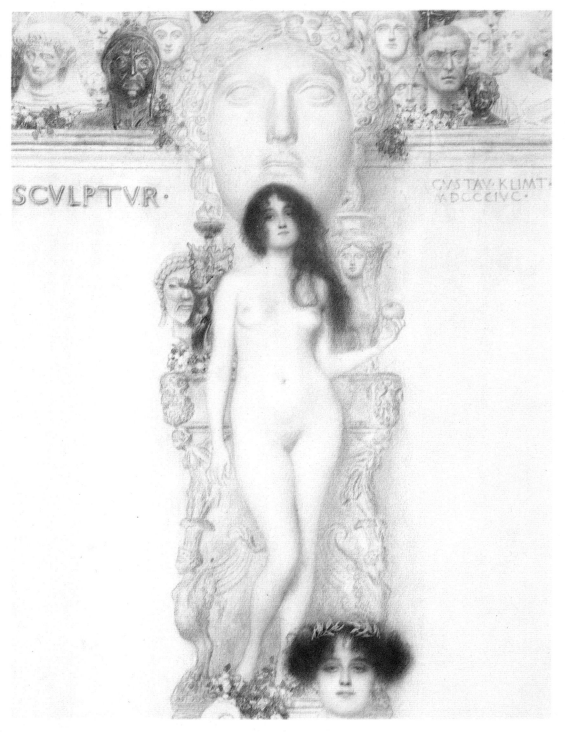

materials, inlays and semi-precious stones would eventually culminate in the *Stoclet Frieze* (1905-1911) in the Palais Stoclet, Brussels. These were often criticized for being only objects of applied art, and thus not works of art on a par with paintings.

The third exhibition of the Secessionists in January 1899 was unusual inasmuch as it allowed a separate room for each contributor. Max Klinger showed his enormous religious-allegorical *Christ on Olympus,* Walter Crane his studies for a frieze based on a Longfellow ballad the *Skeleton in Armor* while Belgian artist Theo Van Rysselberghe showed Pointillist paintings. At this time Klimt was working on *Philosophy* in a studio specially rented for the execution of the University paintings as well as completing the decor for a music room in the town house of Nikolaus von Dumba. These decorations included contrasting 'allegorical' and 'historical' representations of the theme of music in two overdoor paintings.

In the fourth exhibition in March 1899, there were two important works on show by Klimt: *Schubert at the Piano* commissioned by Dumba as an overdoor for his music room and the famous *Nuda Veritas* which bore the apt inscription in the form of a quotation from Schiller: 'If you cannot please all men by your actions and by your art, then please a few. To please everyone is bad. Schiller. Nuda Veritas.' The same year Klimt also painted, for 35,000 crowns, the *Portrait of Serena Lederer,* the wife of August Lederer, Klimt's most important patron.

In January 1900 a sixth exhibition of the Secession was devoted entirely to Japanese art. Despite efforts to bring to

tact with a wider range of painters outside Austria had its influence on Klimt. At the time of the second exhibition Klimt showed his *Portrait of Sonja Knips* and *Pallas Athene. Pallas Athene* shows the influence of Art Nouveau or Jugendstil, as it was called in Germany and Austria, and particularly the work of Franz von Stuck. Stuck had used the image of Athene for his own poster for the seventh Munich secession exhibition as well as for an oil painting. Klimt's version, the third of three representations (Klimt first painted her in a spandrel in the Kunsthistorisohes Museum and again in the Vienna Secession poster), is remarkable for a number of reasons. There is the metal frame designed by the artist and made by his brother Georg (who had also made the great bronze doors for the Secession buildings main entrance). For Klimt, like many of the artists of the Secession, the distinction between painter and craftsman was a barrier that needed to be broken down. Furthermore, there is

the remarkably tiny nude with outstretched arms that appears in the lower left corner and is an image unprecedented in Klimt's work.

Klimt's experiments with decorative

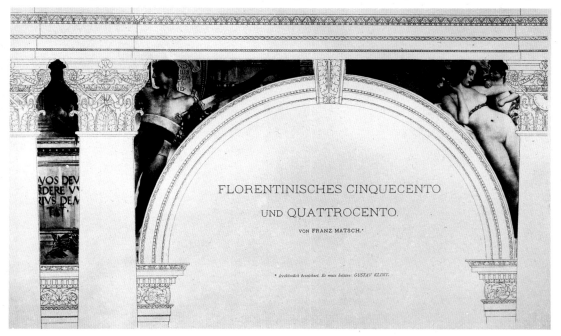

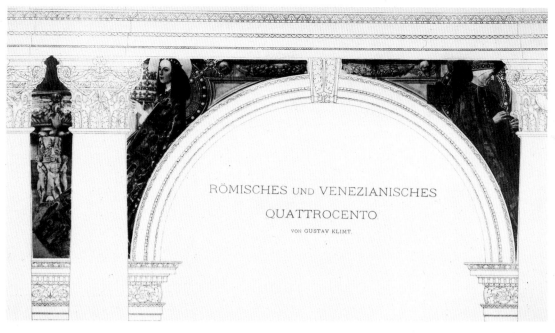

RÖMISCHES UND VENEZIANISCHES
QUATTROCENTO
VON GUSTAV KLIMT.

Austria's attention foreign, exotic and unknown art, the exhibition did not neet with much sympathy from the Viennese public. It was important and valuable however to Klimt as it awakened in him the interest in eastern art which he began to collect. In his possession were paintings and ceramics, sculptures and textiles and these objects were to appear in the backgrounds of his paintings of society

women. In the background of his porrait of *Friederike Maria Beer* appears a design taken from a Korean vase; in the portrait of *Adèle Bloch-Bauer* are oriental horsemen; in the background of the portrait of *Elisabeth Bachofen-Echt* are Chinese figures, while exotic birds in the Japanese style form the background in *Lady with a Fan*.

If the sixth exhibition proved a dis-

appointment to the Secessionists as a whole, it was nevertheless immensely fruitful for Klimt. It was the seventh exhibition in March when *Philosophy* was shown that marked the beginning of the outrage at the University paintings. Although there had been mutterings from the press and public about some of Klimt's earlier work, no-one was quite prepared for what they saw. *Philosophy* was exhibited unfinished with a short explanatory text: 'Left hand group of figures: birth, fertility and decline. On the right: the globe, the cosmic riddle; emerging from below an enlightening figure: knowledge.' The female nude played a prominent role in *Philosophy* and the two other university paintings, not least because the pubic hair of many of the nudes was visible. Klimt was accused of introducing an element of 'ugliness' into some of the figures as an expressive device and this shocked the essentially provincial Viennese and led to charges of obscenity being leveled at Klimt. *Philosophy* and the second university painting *Medicine*, however, were not really original conceptions: the use of allegories and nudes of all ages had became familiar devices in Symbolist works and the most obvious

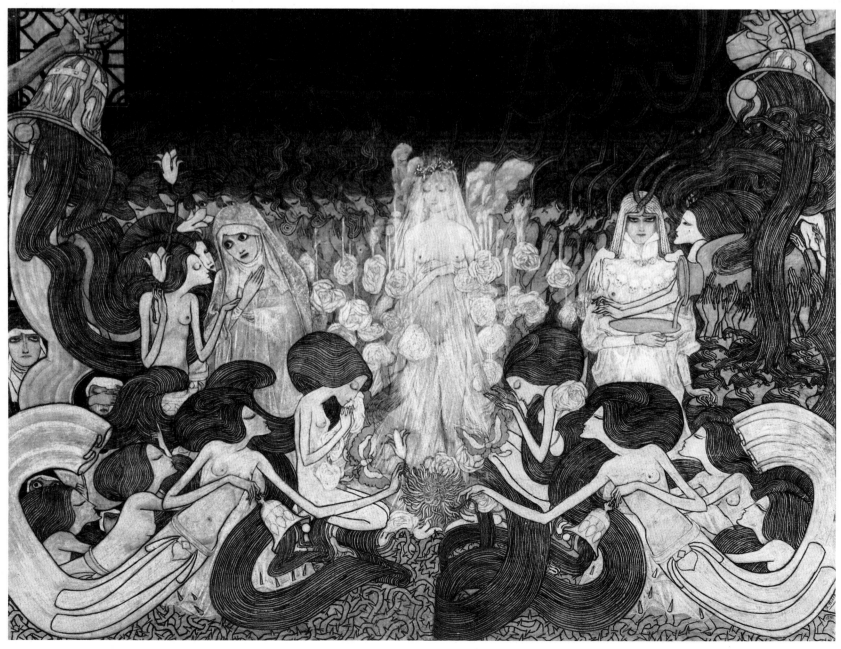

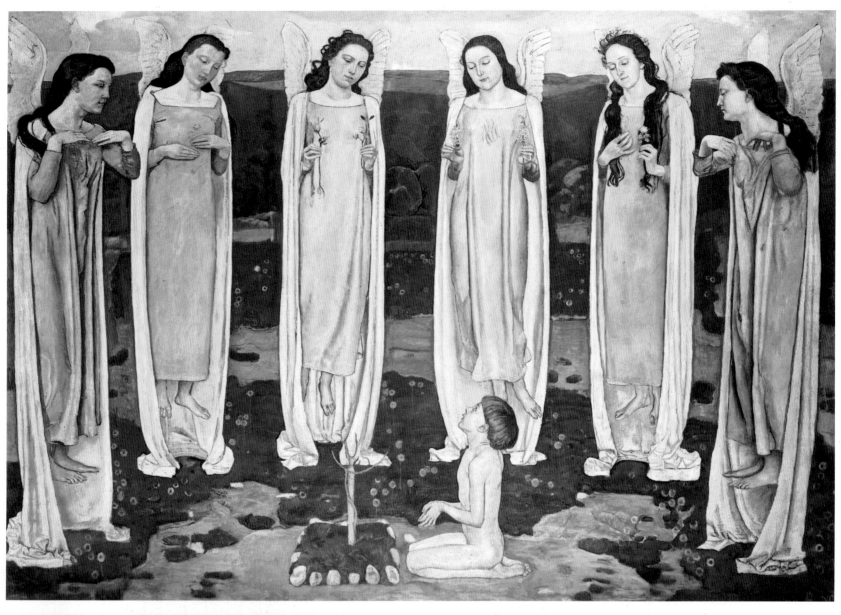

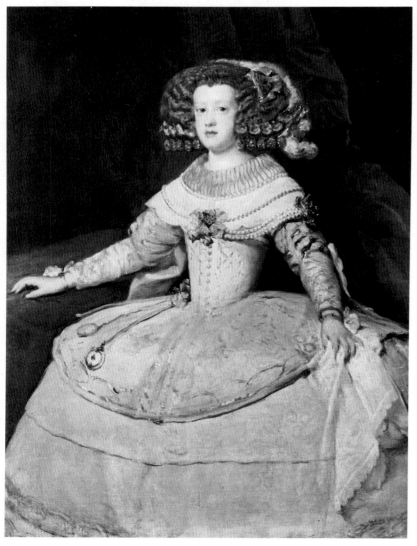

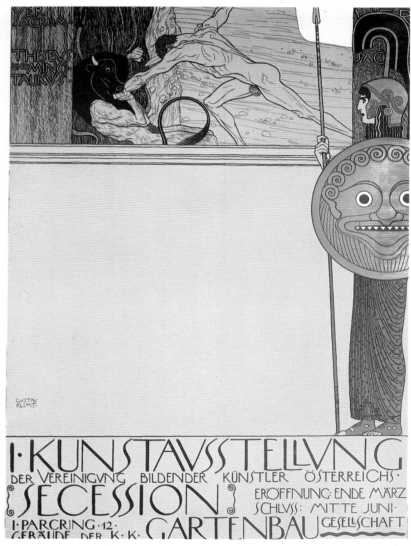

source for Klimt's imagery and individual figures is Rodin's *Gates of Hell* from 1880. In *Philosophy* a struggling chain of 'humanity' is set against the veiled figure which rises from the lowest part of the painting; in *Medicine* the same human chain appears, this time representing the various stages of human development (a theme that Klimt would later return to the *The Three Ages of Woman*) while the figure of Hygieia likewise rising from the bottom of the canvas brings with her physical salvation in the healing powers of medicine. It seems surprising that after all the fuss made about *Philosophy* that Klimt was able to continue on the *Medicine*. The first painting was only on display until the end of March when it went to Paris to be shown at the Austrian Pavillion at the Paris Exposition Universelle. In contract to the artistically narrow views of the Viennese, the French recognized Klimt's achievements and awarded *Philosophy* the Gold medal received for foreign exhibitors. When *Medicine* was exhibited in March 1901 at the tenth Secession Exhibition, it received violent criticism from the daily press. The 'succès de scandale' was such that questions were asked in Parliament and the Minister of Education had to defend the original commissions for the paintings.

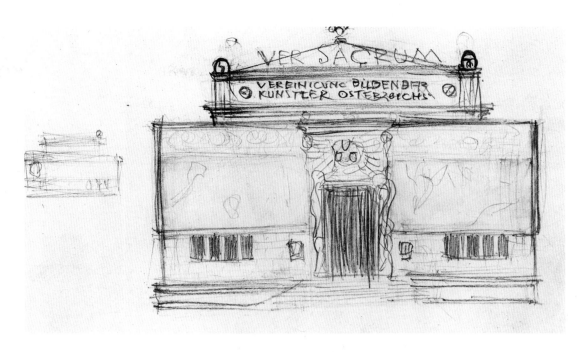

The standing female figure which occupies the upper left-hand part of *Medicine* became the object at the center of the controversy. The Academy authorities demanded that if the figure was to remain female, it was to be clothed. A nude figure would be permissable as long as it was a male nude. In short it was the Academy's view that the painting expressed a preoccupation with female sexuality and as such was offensive.

Where Klimt was acknowledging the

Above left: *The Chosen One* (1893-94) by Ferdinand Hodler.
Above: Klimt's sketch for the proposed exhibition hall for the Secession. The building, known as the *Krautkappel*, was ultimately designed by Josef Olbrich.
Below: Klimt's oil sketch for *Schubert at the Piano*. The finished painting (page 42) was destroyed by fire in 1945.
Below, far left: *Infanta Maria Theresa* by Velázquez.
Below left: The original, uncensored version of Klimt's poster for the Vienna Secession's first exhibition in 1898.

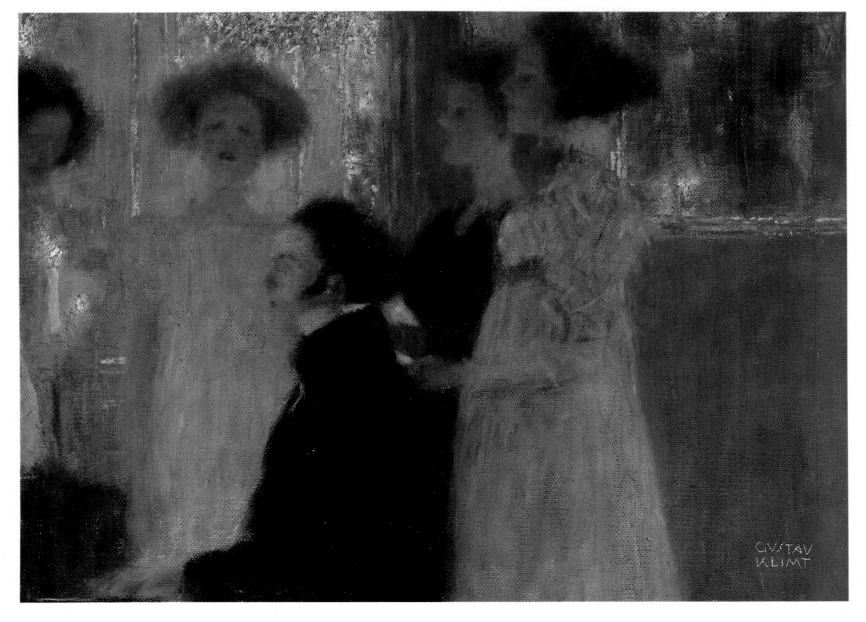

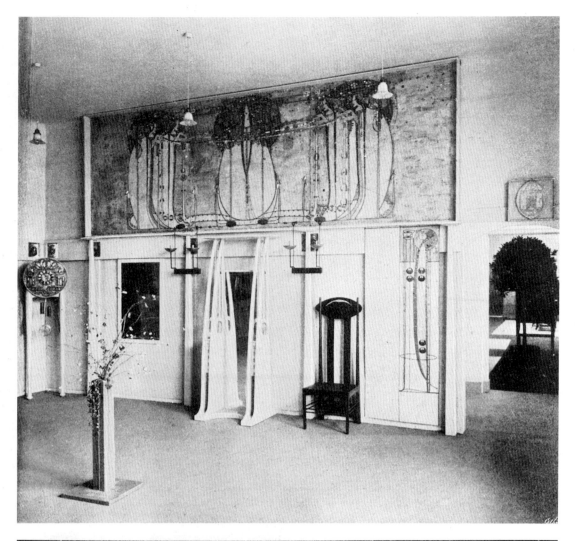

Left: Room design by Charles and Margaret Mackintosh exhibited at the 8th Secession exhibition, 1900.

Right and far right: Compositional sketch and finished version of *Philosophy* (1898-99).

Below: Roller's interior for the 9th Secession show.

golden fabric in *Medicine*, had given way to a new realism of bony nudes, and the 'sfumato' effects of *Philosophy* were now replaced by undulating rhythmic masses. At the top of the painting are the figures representing the law while below, awaiting their punishment, are the figures of an old man and three women. When it was decided that the three paintings would not be placed in the University's Great Hall but in the State Gallery of Modern Art, in 1904 Klimt resigned the commission for the remaining lunettes and, with the help of the industrialist August Lederer, repaid the 30,000 crowns advance he had received for the works. Lederer eventually acquired *Philosophy*, which was built into one of the rooms in his apartment designed by Josef Hoffmann on the Bartensteingasse. *Medicine* and *Jurisprudence* were bought by the artist Kolo Moser. The last occasion on which all three paintings were seen together was at a memorial exhibition in 1943 commemorating the 80th anniversary of Klimt's birth.

In 1945 retreating SS soldiers set fire to the Schloss Immendorf. Many of Klimt's paintings, including *Schubert at the Piano* and *Musik II* which had been evacuated there from the city for safe keeping, were destroyed. Scandals apart, in the years from 1900 to 1902, the Secession exhibitions brought to Vienna many of the major European avant-garde artists including Jan Toorop (1858-1928), a Dutch-Javanese painter. His works, in their abandonment of western spatial concepts, resembled batiks and the surfaces of his pictures are organized by means of undulating lines in complex shallow patterns. Later exhibitions brought to Vienna the work of Ashbee's Guild of Handicrafts and work of the Glasgow four of C R Mackintosh, J H MacNair and Frances and Margaret Macdonald.

In April 1902 the fourteenth Secession Exhibition was dramatically different. This time the exhibition centered on a single work: a monumental sculpture of Beethoven by Max Klinger. Klimt's contribution to the exhibition was the *Beethoven Frieze* (pages 54-57) painted on plaster in casein colors (pigments bound with an emulsion of protein, water and ammonium carbonate) and decorated with gold and semi-precious stones. In a side hall, adjacent to the room where Klinger's sculpture was displayed, Klimt set out a cycle of paintings in three episodes. On the first long wall facing the entrance

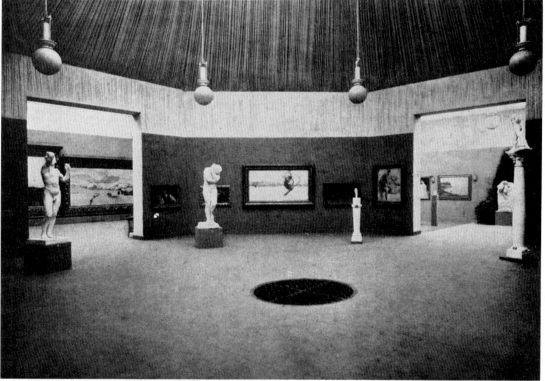

new-found status of women in society at the end of the nineteenth century his critics were expressing their fears. Intellectual and physical reforms had allowed women for the first time to enter the male dominated worlds of culture, science and economics. Women were beginning to take a hand in shaping their own lives independant of their husbands or fathers, and with this came a degree of sexual freedom. Those Viennese entrenched in bourgeois morality no doubt saw in these images of women a sign of revolt against

male domination. Ironically, the final paintings of *Philosophy* and *Medicine* were executed more or less as they had been planned in the original sketches which had been accepted by the Arts Commission of the Ministry of Education.

Jurisprudence, the third of the university paintings, was exhibited in 1903 at the Eighteenth Secession Exhibition. In this painting the naturalism and ornament that had been apparent in Klimt's earlier work, such as the decorative overlay of

14

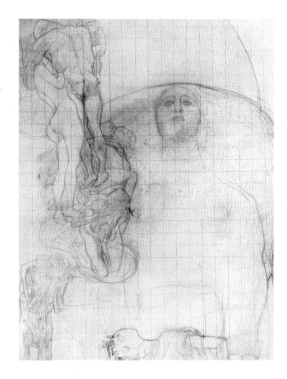

there was the theme of 'longing for happiness': the weak and feeble of mankind appeal for the intervention of the strong (represented here by the Knight) against the hostile powers of debauchery, excess, sickness and madness which are represented on the short wall alongside the giant Typhoes and his three Gorgon daughters. On the second long wall, the 'longing for happiness' finds solace in 'Poetry.' The arts, in Klimt's cycle, lead mankind into an ideal realm and the cycle ends in a climatic chorus of angels in paradise surrounding an embracing couple representing 'The Kiss to the Whole World.' The chorus of angels in this work show the most marked influence of Ferdinard Hodler's *The Chosen One*, where six guardian angels are depicted in a manner that they are neither flying nor resting their feet on the ground since Hodler did not introduce any spatial or atmospheric values. The figure of *Poetry* in the *Beethoven Frieze* harks back to the *Die Musik* paintings and while the torso of the male figure in the embrace under the sun and moon recalls the male torso in *Philosophy*, the embracing couple also look forward to the figures of the *Stoclet Frieze* and to the most famous of Klimt's later works, *The Kiss*.

The Eighteenth Exhibition of the Secession in between November and December of 1903, was entirely devoted to the work of Gustav Klimt. The poster and the cover for the catalogue reproduced Klimt's vignette *Ars*, a further variation on the theme of Athene. On display were 78 works including 30 drawings and studies. In addition to the major paintings *Pallas Athene, Schubert at the Piano* and *Music II* some of Klimt's portraits and early landscapes were shown. Along with the portrait of *Sonja Knips* (1899), the *Portrait of Emilie Flöge* (1902) was shown. Looking at these two portraits, it is possible to see how Klimt had moved away

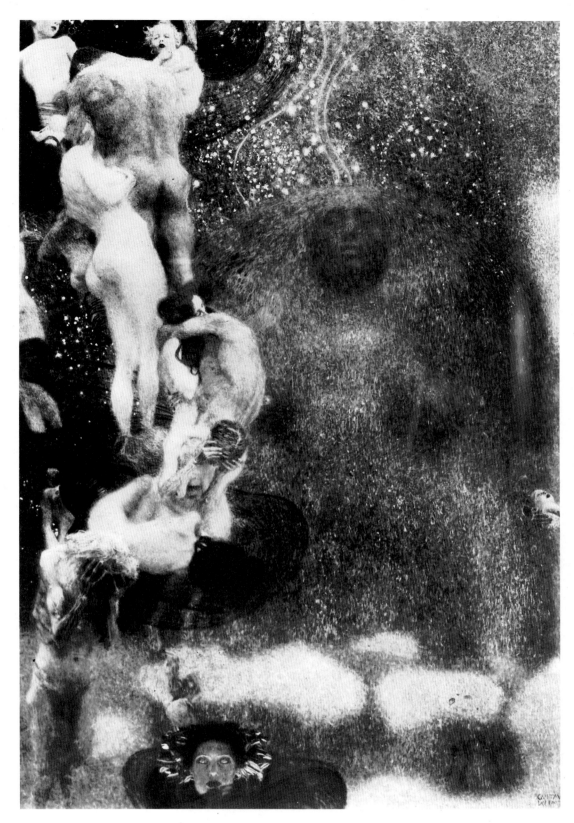

from the impressionist-naturalist manner towards a more geometrical and flatter style. In the later portrait the characeristics that most distinguish Klimt's work – the abstracted treatment of the patterns of fabric – are evident, and while the hands and the face of the sitter are depicted naturalistically, the use of repeating ornamental motifs owes much to Jugendstil design.

In the spring of 1903 Klimt visited Italy and discovered Byzantine art, which was to influence him greatly. From Ravenna he sent his mother a postcard with a picture of the mosaic decorations inside the church of San Vitale. A second journey followed in the winter of that year with his companion, the painter Max Lenz. The mosaics at San Vitale depicting the Emperor Justinian and the Empress

Theodora, each attended by a retinue, combine the characteristics of early Christian art with a tendency toward realism, executed in a monumental style of rare beauty. The enormous impact these mosaics made on Klimt is reflected not only in *Jurisprudence* and in the *Stoclet Frieze* (Klimt's only true mosaic), but also in his later paintings of *The Kiss* (1908) and his portraits of *Fritza Von Riedler* (1905) and *Adèle Bloch-Bauer*.

At the beginning of 1904 the Secession proposed that Austria be represented at the St Louis World Fair by Klimt alone. The heated debate that followed this proposal became so intense that the Secession was eventually prevented from exhibiting at all. The attacks on Klimt for his continued collaboration with Josef Hoffmann which claimed that other painters in

15

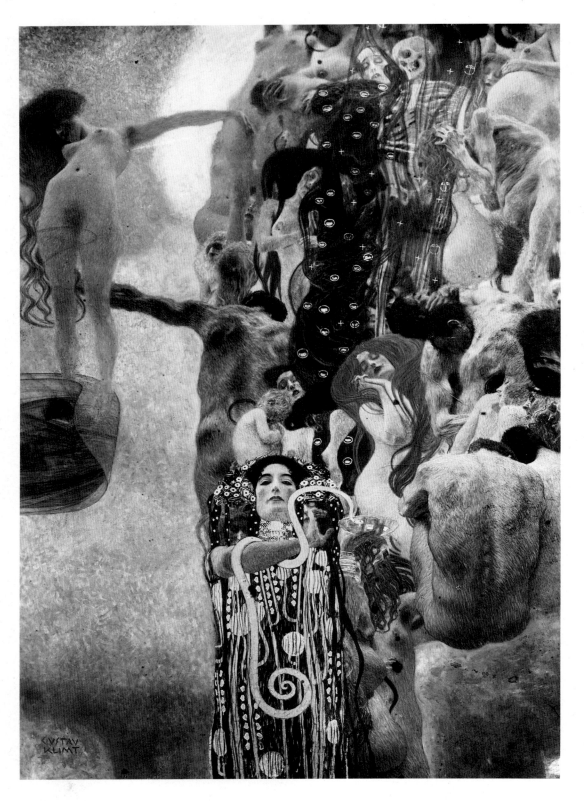

enamel, coral and semi-precious stones against a white marble background was carried out by Leopold Forstner (1878-1936) a member of the Wiener Werkstätte. The two long panels (separated at the entrance end of the dining room by a narrow abstract panel) depict the tree of life. Each of the panels is made up of seven sections, the corresponding panels on each wall being identical, except, for the second panel on the left hand wall where there is the figure of a standing woman, seen in three-quarters profile, who symbolizes *Expectation*. The panel opposite *Expectation* shows an embracing couple, symbolizing *Fulfillment*. On each long wall, in the penultimate panel (that is, towards the entrance to the dining room) in the spreading branches of the Tree of Life is the Magic Bush with its triangular-shaped leaves. On the working drawings for the frieze, Klimt noted that the tree, scrolls and leaves would be in mosaic while the flowers were to be made out of enamel or colored glass. This combination of materials, already hinted at in the use of gold and silver inlay in the *Beethoven Frieze*, anticipates the large-scale mixed media works of 'Klimt's golden years.'

When Klimt and his colleagues resigned from the Secession they found themselves once again without an exhibition space. Nevertheless in 1908 in a prefabricated building designed by Hoffmann erected on a leased area of land off the Lothringerstrasse (today the site of the Konzerthaus) the first Kunstschau was staged. Above the main entrance to the 54 rooms of exhibition space, the original inscription of the Secession building was re-erected: 'Die Zeit ihre Kunst, der Kunstihre Freiheit' (To each age its art, to art its freedom.) In room 22 reserved for Klimt there were three outstanding paintings, the portraits of *Fritza von Riedler* (1907) *Margaret Stonborough-Wittgenstein* (1905) and *Adèle Bloch-Bauer I* (1907). The decorative manner of Klimt's work after the *Stoclet Frieze* is apparent. It is especially evident in the Fritza von Riedler picture, the first of the 'square' portraits of the golden period, with its repeated 'eye' motif on the chair on which the privy councillor's wife is seated and in the semi-circular mosaic headdress. The headdress device seems to have been taken from Velázquez's portraits of the Spanish royal family which were on display in Vienna at The Kunsthistorisches Museum. While the portrait of *Adèle Bloch-Bauer I* had a strong two-dimentional organization and fabulous gold decoration, the earlier Wittgenstein portrait can be viewed more as a traditional painting, halfway between

Above: *Medicine* (1901), the second of the University murals.

Right: *Jurisprudence* (1903).

the group were bing overlooked, led to the start of tensions within the group: the Klimt group which included Hoffmann, Otto Wagner, Kolo Moser and Carl Moll and the Nur Maler (pure painters) led by Engelhart. In 1905 following a debate on the running by Carl Moll of a gallery as a commercial outlet for Secession artists, the Klimt group lost by one vote. Klimt and some of the leading members of the Secession promptly tendered their resignations and quit the Secession. Viennese modernism was now left to Klimt and his friends in the newly founded Wiener Werkstätte. The attacks on Klimt, however, did not interfere with his work. In 1904 he was at the Great Art Exhibition in Dresden showing works including *Gold Fish* and *The Golden Knight* (life, a struggle), while in Munich at the first exhibition of the Deutscher Künstlerbund, the *Procession of the Dead* was shown. With

these paintings we see the beginnings of the strongly two-dimensional work with gold paint and the allegorical use of the motif of floating as an expression of suffering. The skeletal shapes, which were inspired by Toorop, that appear in *Procession of the Dead* were subsequently to be developed by Egon Schiele.

In the same year, 1904, Josef Hoffmann, one of the founder-members of the Wiener Werkstätte was commissioned to built a town house in Brussels for the Belgian financier Adolphe Stoclet and his wife, Suzanne. The Palais Stoclet, Hoffmann's magnum opus, was designed to show off the works of art collected by the Stoclets as well as to entertain the artistic and cultural élite of Europe. Klimt was commissioned to design the dining-room frieze to be carried out in mosaic, now known simply as the *Stoclet Frieze*. The frieze, executed in gold and silver, with

16

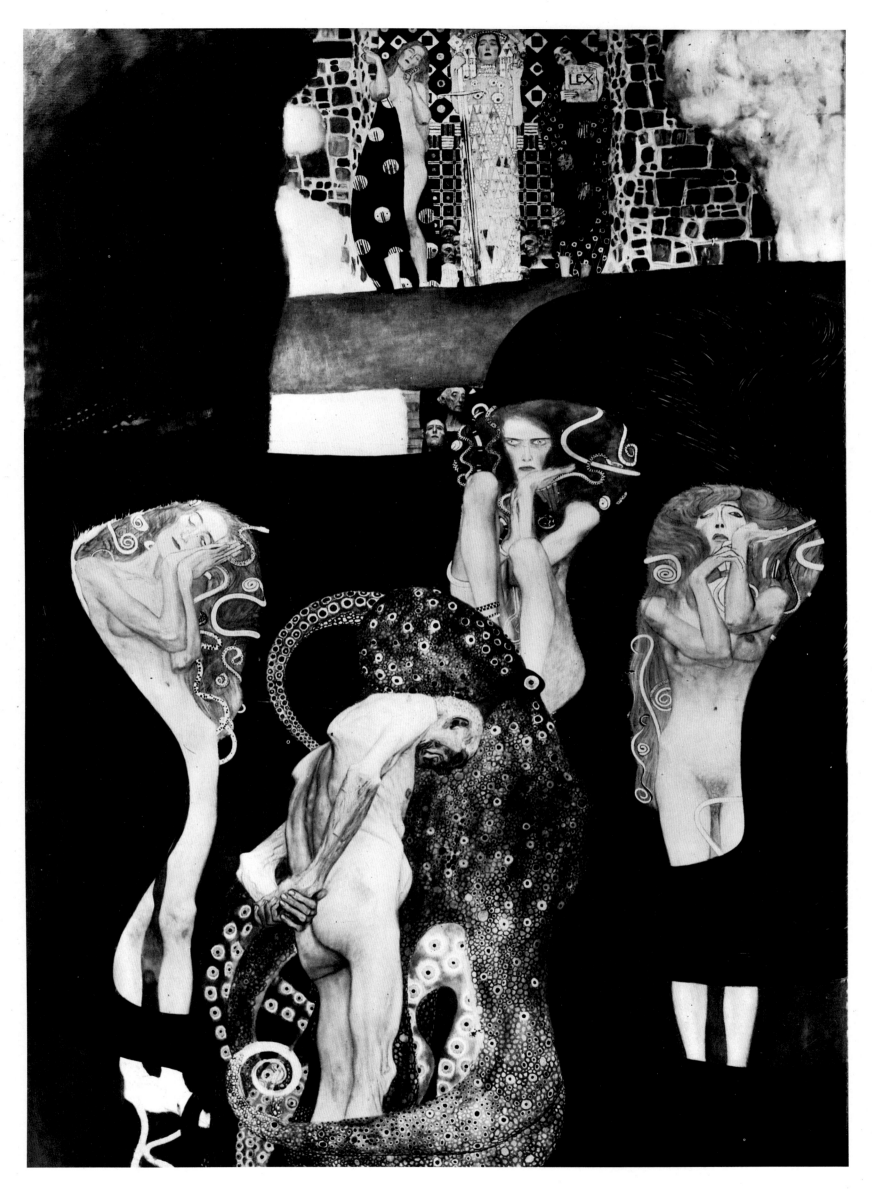

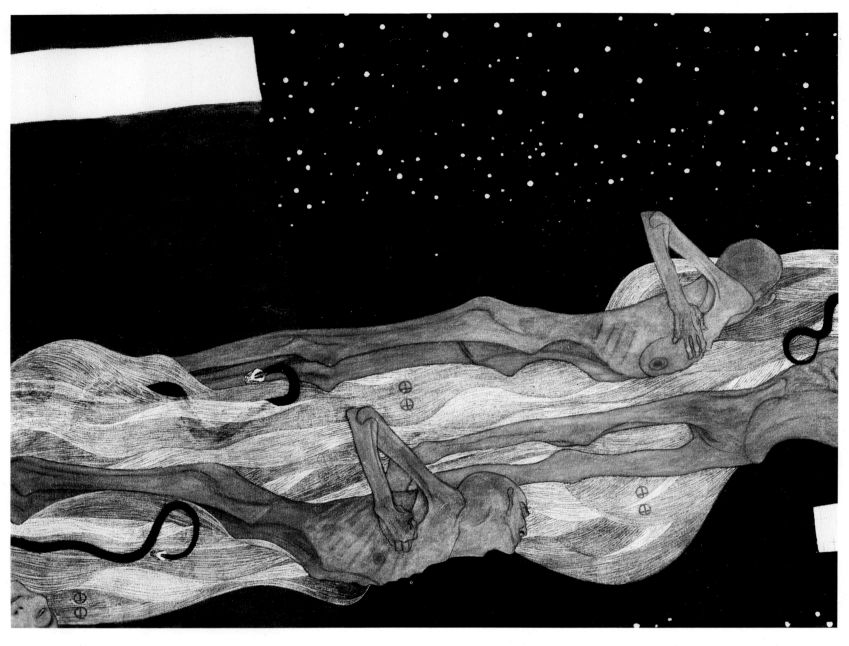

Above: Klimt's *Procession of the Dead* (1903) destroyed in 1945.

Above right: Max Klinger's monumental polychrome sculpture *Beethoven*, the center piece of the 14th Secession exhibition in April 1902.

Far right: Klimt's study for the figures of the *Hostile Powers* for the *Beethoven Frieze*.

Right: The *Hostile Powers* from the *Beethoven Frieze*, 1902.

the impressionism of the *Sonja Knips* portrait of 1898 and the more decorative manner of his work after the *Stoclet Frieze*. The architectural motifs in the background of the Wittgenstein portrait were later to develop into the almost complete breakdown of foreground and background into very shallow pictorial space.

The central item of Klimt's display was, however, *The Kiss* (1907-08); the climax of his mosaic style is a work of sheer decorative splendor in its combination of oils and golden decoration. The stylization of the clothing, first apparent in the portrait of *Emilie Flöge* and then in the figures of the *Stoclet Frieze*, is here taken to its extreme: the clothes are now translated into surface patterns. *The Kiss* is also the most

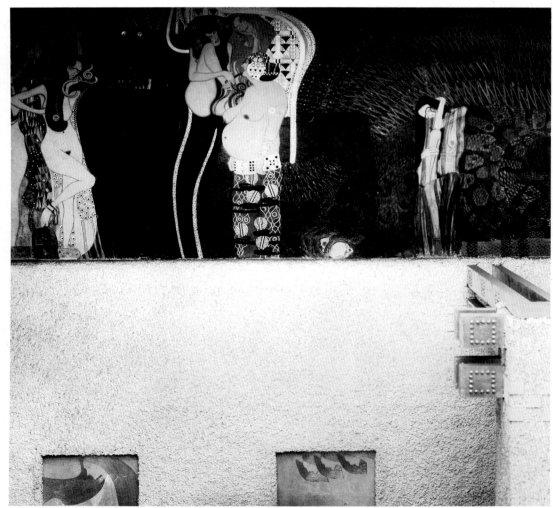

18

elaborate working of the theme of the embrace which appeared in Klimt's work as early as the symbolist-inspired *Love* of 1895. In spite of the dazzling and brilliant appearance of *The Kiss,* there is within it a certain tension or 'angst.' Often considered as the symbol of union between man and woman, the woman's hand around the man's neck however is not depicted in a relaxed pose, but shown cramped, almost into a fist; and although he has bent to kiss her, she has turned away, offering her cheek and not her lips. Although physically close the woman remains remote. A similar tension also appears in Klimt's portraits: they are not essentially flattering for Klimt has not 'beautified' them. Here again the hands of his sitters are often clasped or twisted together. Even in what appears to be in the most 'tender' of paintings, *Love,* behind the couple lurk sinister and grotesque faces.

The very first of Klimt's paintings were concerned with women, both portraits of his family and relations and in allegorical subjects. Initially it was women's beauty that attracted him, but there was a further aspect that interested Klimt, women's sexuality, which became a varied theme in his work. In an age and society where sexuality was never mentioned except in scientific circles, it was nevertheless assumed that men would gain their sexual experiences with prostitutes or perhaps with their servants. That women should have the same urges or need for physical affection as men offended the notion of the sanctity of woman. It is not surprising that the novels of Emile Zola and Gustave Flaubert were considered immoral, that Isadora Duncan's expressive dancing should provoke scandal or that Klimt be accused of painting pornography.

The attempts by writers and artists to open up the subject of women's role in society and their sexuality were added to by psychologists like Sigmund Freud who had already made his name with *Studies in Hysteria* (1895) and the *Interpretation of Dreams* (1900). Freud's belief was that our subconscious desires were the motivation for all our decisions and actions. The subconscious, in Freud's view, was govered by the 'libido,' the desire for sexual gratification which be believed was present in us from infancy. A repressed libido could not only lead to psychological disorders but also to physical illnesses. Although only six hundred copies of the *Interpretation of Dreams* were printed, Klimt no doubt was aware of the sexual fixation in Freud's writing through the close-knit artistic and literary circles in Vienna: Hermann Bahr, a literary adviser to the Secession magazine *Ver Sacrum* (on which Klimt was an editoral board member) had a copy.

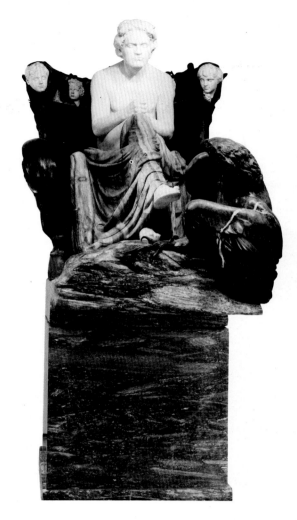

Klimt's own sexual vitality and his many love affairs are well known and in numerous drawings and paintings he expressed his belief in sexuality as the divine force of human existence in its pursuit of happiness. Reflecting this belief some of Klim's women are seductresses, like Danae, 'available' even while she sleeps; others have become powerful creatures

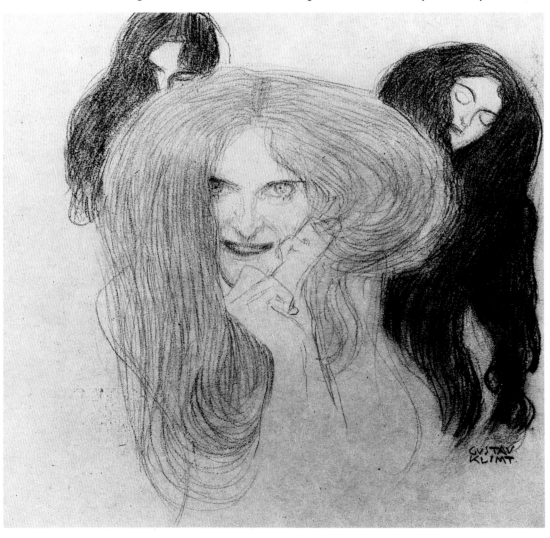

capable of destroying men, like Judith and *Salome* who demands the head of her beloved because he will not submit to her will.

At the exhibition of the Kunstschau in 1909, in addition to works by the French Nabis (Pierre Bonnard, Edouard Vuillard and Maurice Denis), the Fauves (Henri Matisse and Maurice de Vlaminck) and the young Egon Schiele, Klimt showed some of his most recent works including *Judith II (Salome),* as well as an earlier painting, *Hope I,* here exhibited for the first time. This painting, one of the most individual and striking images of pregnancy, formed part of the collection of Fritz Wärndorfer, the original financial backer of the Wiener Werkstätte, who had a shrine constructed so as to have the painting behind locked doors.

The two Kunstschau exhibitions were to prove financially disastrous for the organizers and Hoffmann's exhibition rooms were subsequently demolished. Many commentors have seen the years between the closure of the Kunstschau in 1909 and the outbreak of World War I as an artistically and culturally barren period where Vienna was eclipsed by Berlin as the cultural city of Europe. While many of the leading artists resident in Vienna slowly began to quit the city, after the completion of the *Stoclet Frieze* Klimt retreated into increasing isolation and his work shows the increasing influence of foreign styles. Klimt's landscapes returned to a style loosely based on

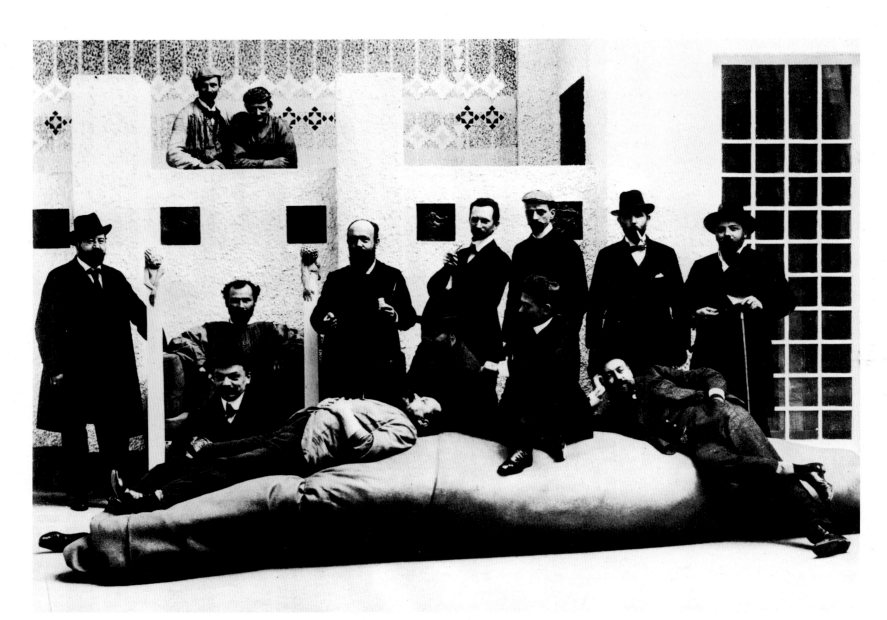

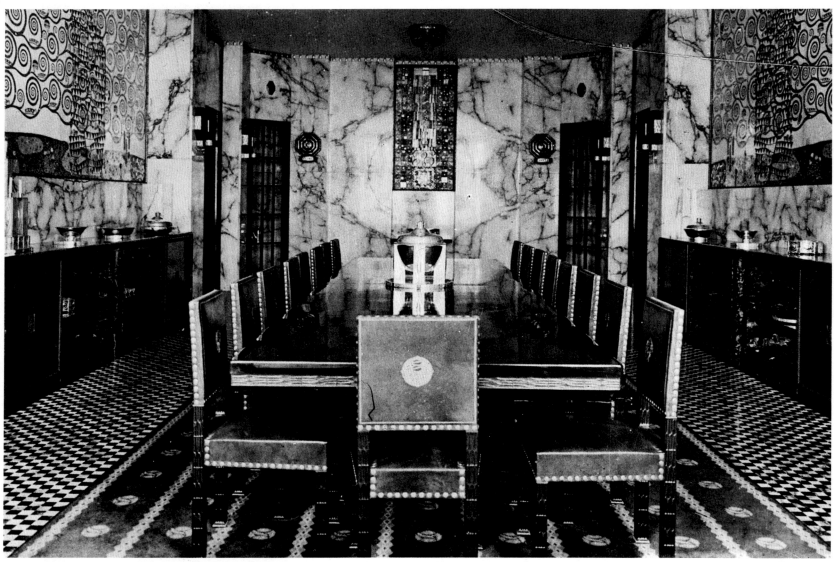

the Neo-Impressionist divisionist technique and his portraits betray the influence of the Nabis and of Matisse.

The pattern of Klimt's life became less varied: in the summer he vacationed at Attersee, a lake resort popular with the Viennese. For more than ten years Klimt and the Flöge sisters had travelled to Attersee, staying first in Lizlberg, then Kammerl and finally, between 1914 and 1916, at Weissenbach. The only exceptions to the summers at Attersee were trips to Lake Garda in 1913 and Mayhofen in 1917.

The rest of the year Klimt spent in Vienna where his working day was organized by a srict routine. After breakfast at the Café Tiroli he went to his studio to work without interruption. From 1904 Klimt began regular nude drawings of several professional models often present together in his studio. During brief interludes in his painting sessions Klimt would request his models from an adjacent waiting room and would make rapid sketches of them. Increasingly his explorations of female sexuality gave way to heightened voyeurism.

The area around Attersee is the subject of many of Klimt's landscapes, in particular the Schloss Kammer, painted from a variety of viewpoints. While some of the

Above left: Members of the Vienna Secession in a group photograph at the 14th exhibition, 1902.

Left: The Palais Stoclet dining room.

Below: One of Klimt's numerous drawings of female sleeping nudes.

landscapes are indebted to the French Post-Impressionists, some of the views of the Schloss Kammer, with their thicker colors and twisting rhythmic forms, betray the influence of Van Gogh. As an artist who would have made numerous studies and drawings for his portraits and allegorical compositions, it seems strange that Klimt should paint these landscapes without preliminary sketches and that as a confirmed studio painter, that he should have painted *en plein air* at all. It is possible that his notebooks, which he always carried with him, would have provided us with a greater insight into his landscapes and motivation. These notebooks however have disappeared, possibly destroyed.

The only interruption to his routine that Klimt allowed to his daily work in the studio – in 1911 he moved to a new studio in Vienna – was his annual (through occasionally twice yearly) visit to the home of the Primavesi family near Olmitz. Otto Primavesi, a banker and financier was originally the patron of Josef Hoffmann (who seems to have initiated these visits) and who eventually took over the funding of the Wiener Werkstätte after Wärndorfer had left for the United States. Each year Primavesi and his wife entertained a wide circle of friends with a Schweindelfest (a sort of large barbecue). In addition to buying several examples of Klimt's work, the Primavesis commissioned two family portraits, of their daughter *Mäda Primavesi* and of Mäda's mother, Eugenia.

As Europe moved into war, portraiture

occupied a great deal of Klimt's time, and he often made use of his collection of oriental art to provide the background to his sitters. In 1915 Klimt temporarily abandonned strong colors and produced two portraits in green and gray tones: *Barbara Flöge* (Emilie's mother) and *Charlotte Pulitzer* (the mother of Serena Lederer). But a further important change in Klimt's style was to come about at the beginning of 1917. The emphasis on pattern, decoration and strong color is still evident, but there is an increasing concern with more geometrical compositions and forms. In the *Baby* (also called the *Cradle*) Klimt uses a triangular shape as the basis of his composition. In this period the main influence on Klimt's work came from Egon Schiele (1890-1918) whose work displayed an exaggerated geometry. In Klimt's *Leda* (1917), the pose of the central figure, in particular, is a re-working of schiele's *Danae* of 1909 and the triangular composition of Klimt's later works can be found in Schiele's *Death and the Maiden* (1915).

The importance Klimt was giving to the abstract elements of the compositions and the new direction he was taking in his art were tragically cut short and several convasses were left unfinished in his studio. Following his return to Vienna in January 1918 after a Christmas journey to Romania, Klimt suffered a stroke. His condition was aggravated by the influenza epidemic that was savaging Europe after World War I. Gustav Klimt died on 6 February 6 1918 and was buried in the Hietzing Cemetery in Vienna.

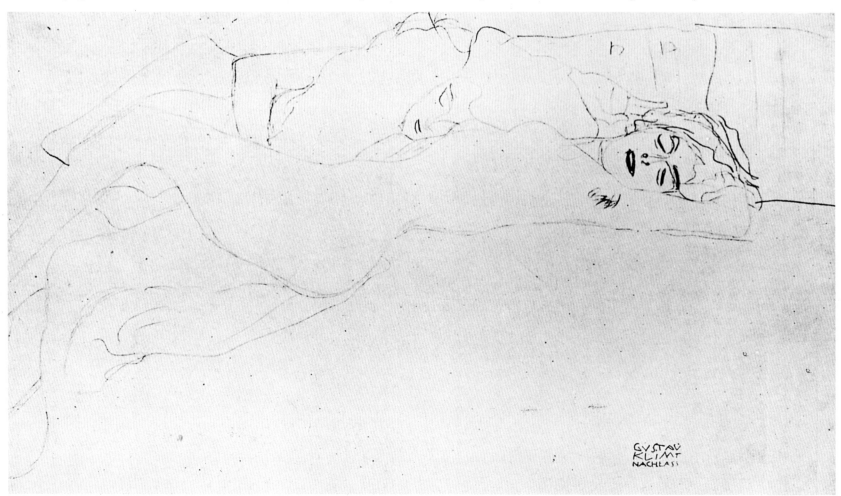

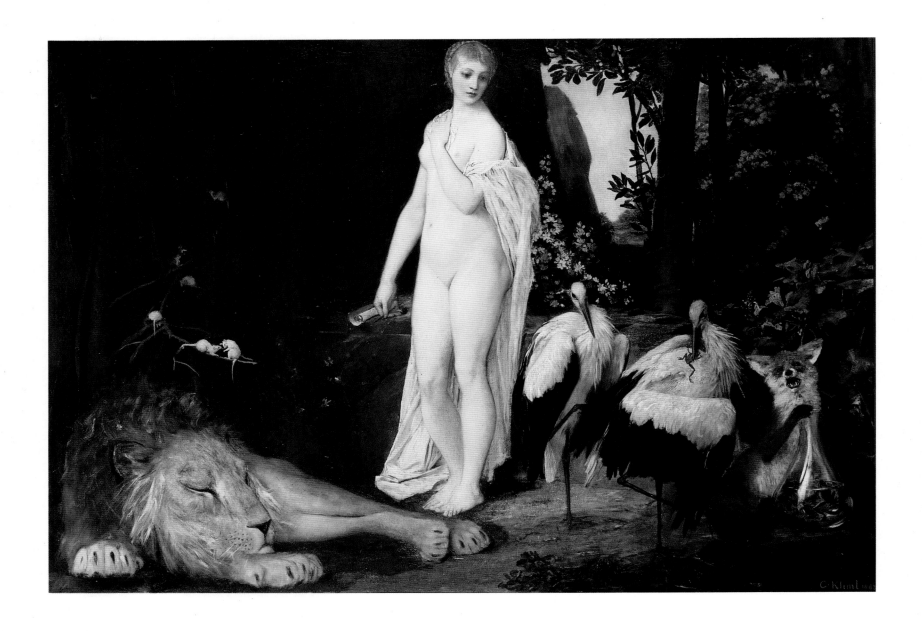

Fable, 1883
Oil on canvas
33¼×46 inches (84.5×117cm)
Historisches Museum der Stadt Wien,
Vienna

In 1881 Klimt was commissioned by Martin Gerlach to supply designs for a publication *Allegories and Emblems*. The three-volume work comprised 'original designs by the most outstanding modern artists, and reproductions of ancient guild emblems, with modern heraldic figures in renaissance style.' Other important contributors to the publication were Max Klinger and Franz von Stuck.

The aim of *Allegories and Emblems* was to rival the allegories used in Renaissance, Baroque and Rococo art with new figures

representing the modern achievements of government, trade, and technology introduced to complement the 'older' allegorical figures of love, the times of the day, and the seasons. While some of Klimt's earlier designs for the publication such as the *Four Seasons* and *Youth* show the influence of his teacher Ferdinand Laufberger, the later oil paintings of *Fable* and Idyll (1884; page 23) betray the influence of Hans Makart.

Reflecting the academic style of the period, *Fable* presents a wooded scene in

which stands the figure of Fable, a nude female figure whose drapery has slipped from her shoulder. Everything in the picture appears to have been frozen: the figure of Fable is rather wooden and lifeless, almost like a statue. No more animated are the sleeping lion and the two storks, and even the frog caught in the beak of one of the birds has stopped wriggling. In the following year Klimt would succeed in making his figures more convincing by representing them truly as statues.

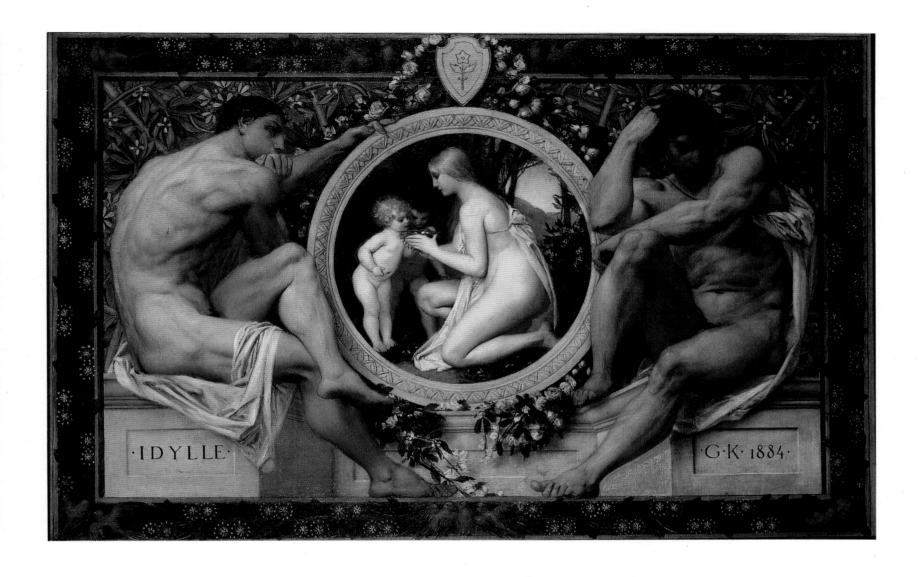

Idyll, 1884

Oil on canvas
19×29 inches (49.5×73.5cm)
Historisches Museum der Stadt Wien,
Vienna

A companion painting to *Fable*, painted
for Martin Gerlach's *Allegories and
Emblems*, *Idyll* was painted during a
period when Klimt was copying the
works of the old masters. Against a background of intertwining branches – remarkably like a William Morris pattern –
are two nude male figures strongly influenced by Michelangelo. The two
figures are set on grisaille bases bearing

the title and the artist's initials and date.
Apart from their hair, eyes and mouths,
the bodies are painted a uniform yellow-
ish tone. The effect is of human heads on
the bodies of statues, an effect that Klimt
was subsequently to develop in his portraits and allegorical compositions. In a
tondo with a stucco frame the figure of
Idyll kneels before her children offering
them a drink.

Auditorium in the Old Burgtheater, Vienna, 1888

Gouache on paper
$32\frac{1}{4} \times 36\frac{1}{4}$ inches (82×92 cm)
Historisches Museum der Stadt Wien,
Vienna

It was not until around 1899 that Klimt fully refined his artistic style, moving from the historicism of works such as the decorations for the staircases of the Burgtheater to the avant-garde allegories of the University commissions. Until that time Klimt continued to work as the 'heir' to the tradition of Hans Makart, the most influential Viennese painter of the 1880s.

Paintings such as the *Auditorium in the Old Burgtheater, Vienna* met with great approval from the academic authorities: in 1888 Klimt was awarded the highest artistic honor, the Gold Cross of Merit, by the emperor Franz Josef for the cycle of paintings depicting the history of the theater, and in 1890, for this large gouache painting of the audience in the theater, he received the Emperor's Prize of 400 guilden.

In spite of first appearances, the *Auditorium in the Old Burgtheater* displays that peculiar realism and sense of artificiality, especially in the treatment of the physiognomies of contemporary Viennese, that was increasingly to play an important role in Klimt's work as he moved towards a more decorative symbolism. Furthermore, the format of this painting looks forward to the square canvasses of many of his landscapes, portraits and allegorical compositions.

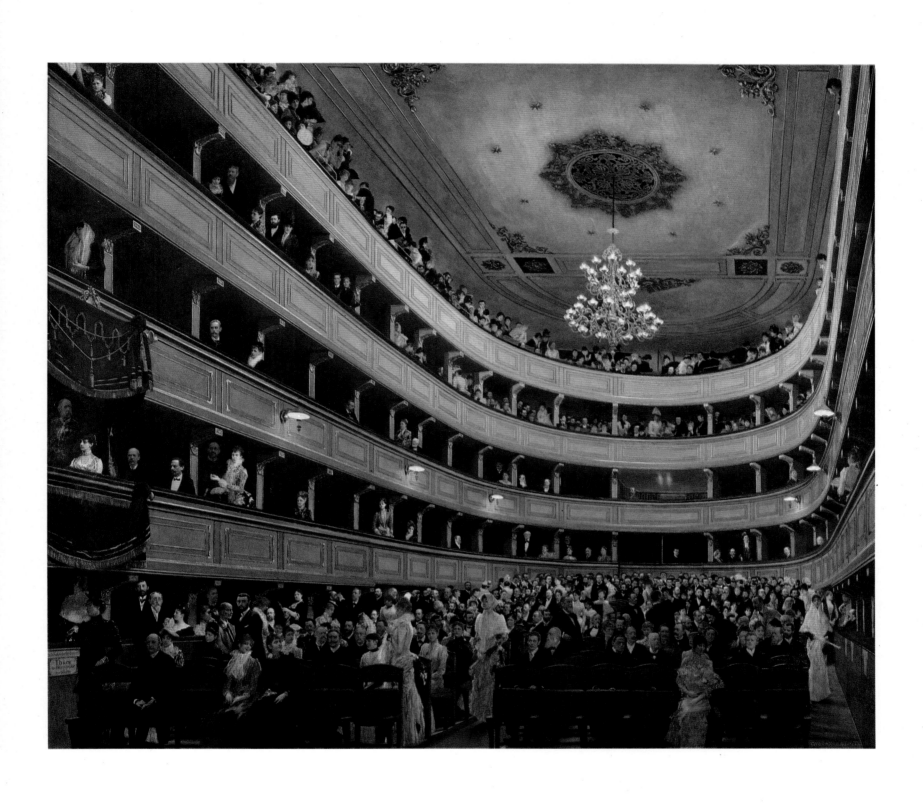

Portrait of the Pianist and Piano Teacher Joseph Pembauer, 1890

Oil on canvas
$27\frac{3}{16} \times 21\frac{5}{8}$ inches (69×55cm)
Tiroler Landesmuseum Ferdinandeum,
Innsbruck

Between 1888 and 1890 Gustav, his brother Ernst, and their colleague Franz Matsch built up such a reputation that they were invited to several major artistic and cultural events. One such event was the unveiling of the memorial in Bolzano to the twelfth-century Minnesinger and poet to the Dukes of Babenburg, Walter von der Vogelweide. Vogelweide's elegies mourning the vanished years of his life and questioning their reality were influential on a number of later writers in Austria including the philosopher Ernst Mach in the 1880s and the neo-Classicist Grillparzer who would later be paraphrased by Schnitzler and Hugo von Hoffmannsthal.

At the unveiling ceremony, a mutual friend of the 'Klimt studio,' Georg Reimer, spoke in honor of the pianist, composer and teacher Joseph Pembauer (1848-1923), who was responsible for organizing the ceremony. The speech gave rise to the idea of a 'Pembauer Society.' The members met each Thursday at the Löwenbräu tavern in Vienna and in 1890 Klimt painted this portrait of Pembauer to hang in their meeting room at the tavern.

Of all of Klimt's paintings, it is possible to call to mind only three portraits with male sitters: *Schubert at the Piano* (page 42), *Hofburg Actor Josef Lewinsky as Carlos* and this portrait of Pembauer. Klimt's oeuvre is dominated by the image of woman.

The portrait of Pembauer is remarkable also for its wooden frame (believed to have been designed by Klimt) and the photographic realism of the features of the sitter. Behind Pembauer's head is a golden lyre, symbolic of the sitter's musical passion. At the top left of the frame there appears a Greek figure carrying a lyre – a figure we will see again in *Die Musik I* and the *Beethoven Frieze*.

26

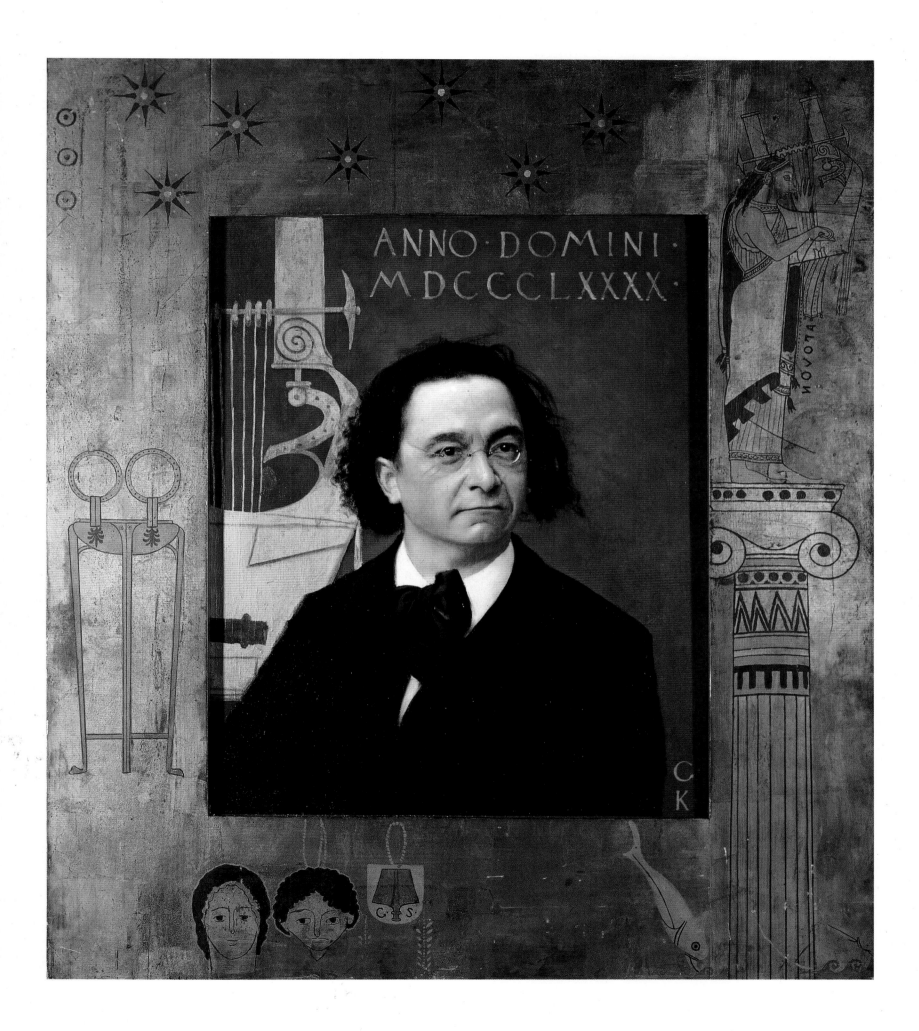

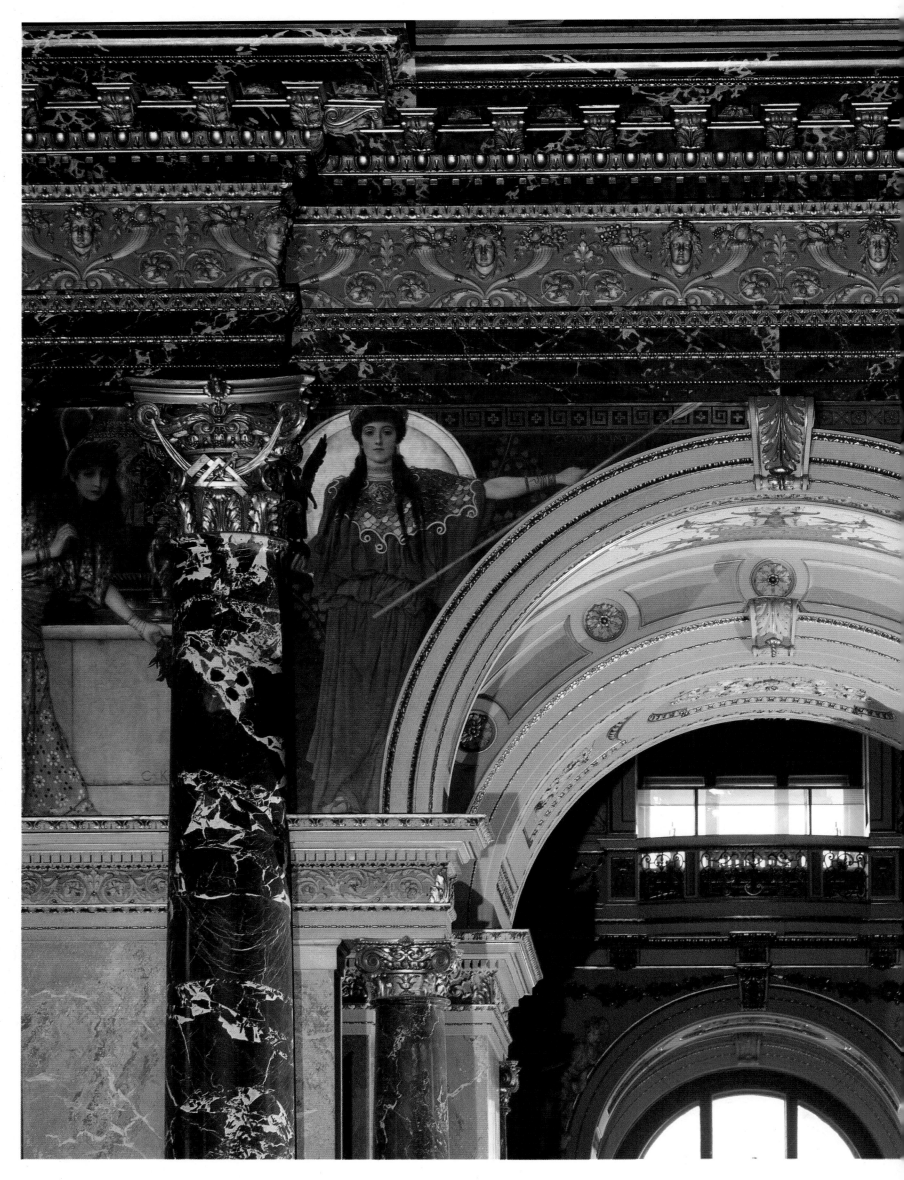

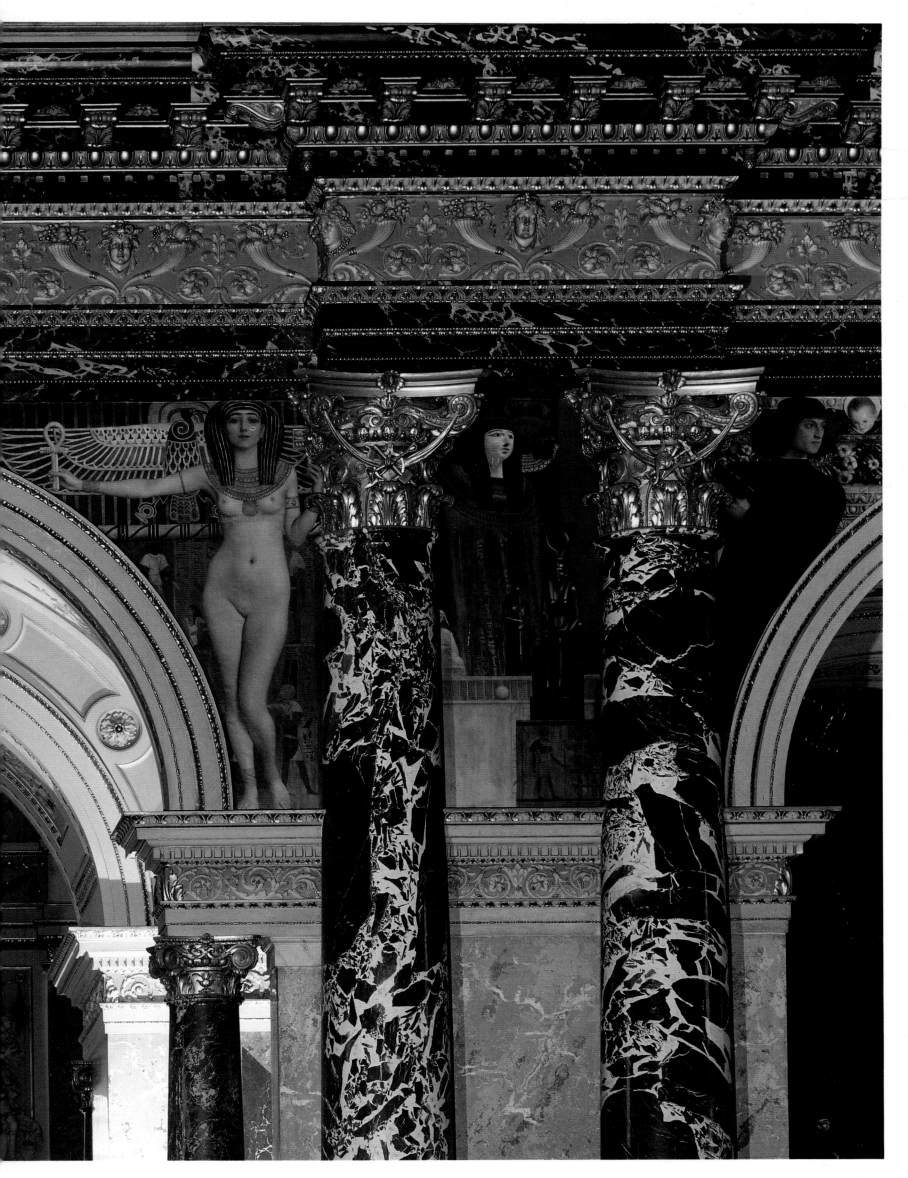

Ancient Greek I and II, Ancient Egyptian I and II,
1890-91
Oil on stucco
Intercolumnar paintings, c.90½×31½ inches (c.230×80cm)
Spandrel paintings, c.90½×90½ inches (c.230×80cm)
Kunsthistorisches Museum, Vienna

In 1890, following their earlier success with the paintings for the staircase at the Burgtheater, the 'Klimt studio' – Gustav, his brother Ernst and the academic painter Franz Matsch – were assigned the commission to complete the decorations in the stairwell of the Kunsthistorisches Museum in Vienna, a task the studio had inherited from Makart who had died in 1884. While the ceiling panel was to be painted by Michael Munkascy, the Klimt studio painted the forty spandrel and intercolumnar pictures. Of these, Gustav painted eleven pictures which have as their subject the development of art from ancient Egypt to the sixteenth century, a suitable theme for an art museum.

By this time, however, Klimt was moving further away from the academic conception of painting and began the representation of figures in a strictly frontal aspect on a gold background. In addition, we see here the first appearance of the femme fatale type in the *Girl from Tanagra*.

On completion, the stairwell paintings attracted considerable favorable attention and led the Arts Commission of the Ministry of Education to consider the studio for the paintings to decorate the Great Hall of Vienna University.

Portrait of a Lady (Frau Heymann?), 1894
Oil on wood
15⅓×9 inches (39×23cm)
Historisches Museum der Stadt Wien, Vienna

Klimt's portraits, probably the best known of his works, have never really attracted much attention for the accuracy with which Klimt portrayed his sitters. Instead, the emphasis has been placed on the formal qualities and development. Even in his early portraits such as this, Klimt never really defines any location or spatial structure. The exception is the *Portrait of Sonja Knips* (1898; page 37), where we sense that the young woman is in a garden. The location is replaced by ornamental areas, in *Portrait of a Lady*, with an art nouveau wallpaper. Gradually the use of decorative elements led to a merging of bodies into the background, while the sitters head and hands remained naturalistically portrayed.

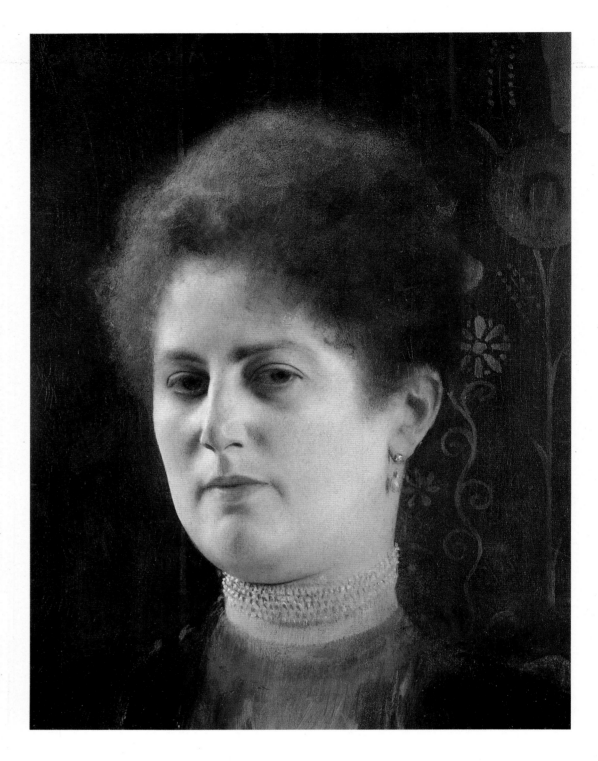

Love, 1895
Oil on canvas
23⅝×17⅓ inches (60×44cm)
Historisches Museum der Stadt Wien, Vienna

In *Love*, love is translated by Klimt into a dreamlike – or nightmarish – world in which grotesques lurk in a vision above the two lovers. One of the earliest workings of the theme of the 'embrace,' *Love* was published as a color reproduction in the series of Martin Gerlach's *Allegories* in 1895, and betrays the influence of Jugendstil painting along with traces of Romanticism and the German Nazarenes. The melancholy tone of the painting, emphasizing that the sweetness of love cannot prevent the occurance of the threats of jealousy and death, is comparable in many ways to the mood of Arthur Schnitzler's stories.

Schnitzler was a young doctor who, besides publishing a tract on hypnosis, had also produced short, one-act plays, later united in *Anatole*, written between 1888 and 1891. The Viennese writer par excellence, Schnitzler in *Anatole* sketched typical characters and situations among the lighthearted yet fashionably melancholic youth of Viennese society: the charming, sensitive yet self-absorbed, lazy and somewhat ruthless man-about-town Anatole; the sweet Süsse Mädel (Austria's equivalent of a 'grisette'), a tenderhearted girl who is deserted; and the femme fatale – beautiful (and married), manipulative and faithless – a perfect partner for the passionate yet heartless Anatole. The hero does not die, but marries, spelling the end not of his mortal life, but of a way of life'.

30

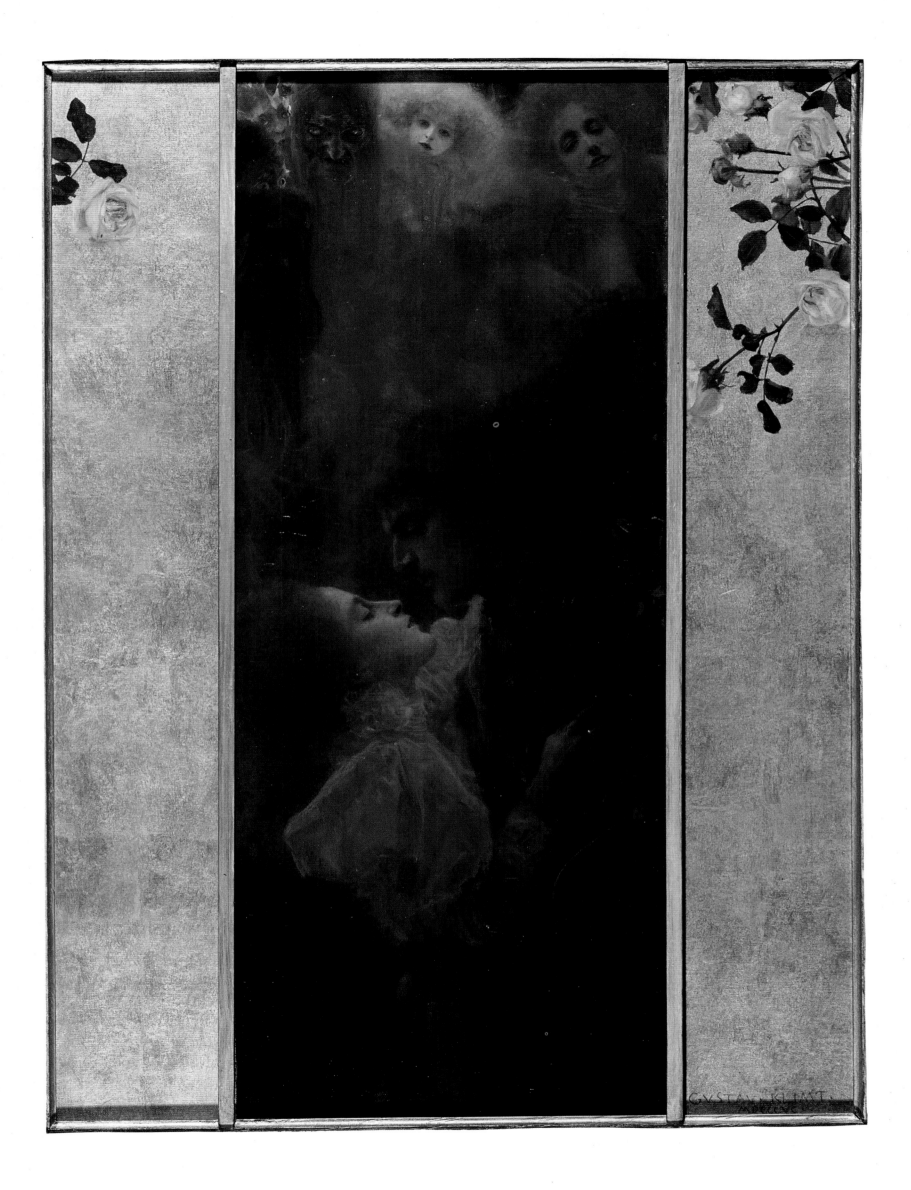

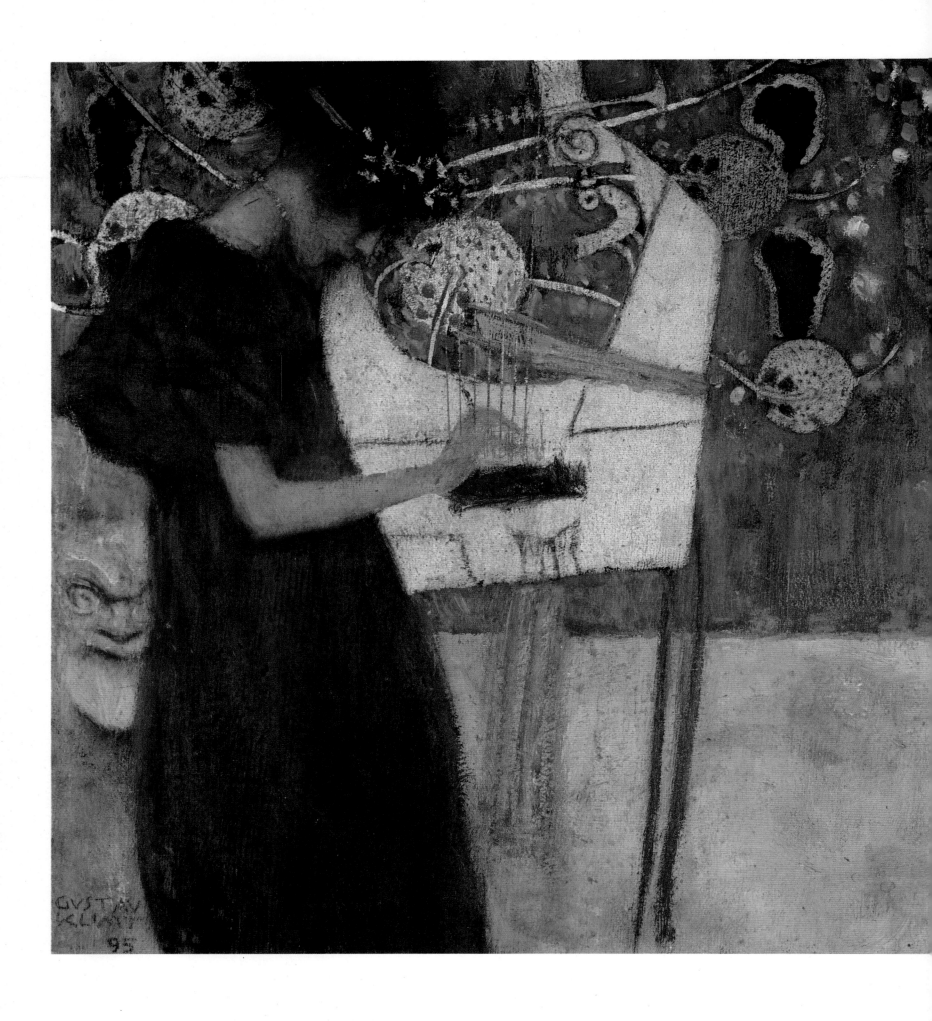

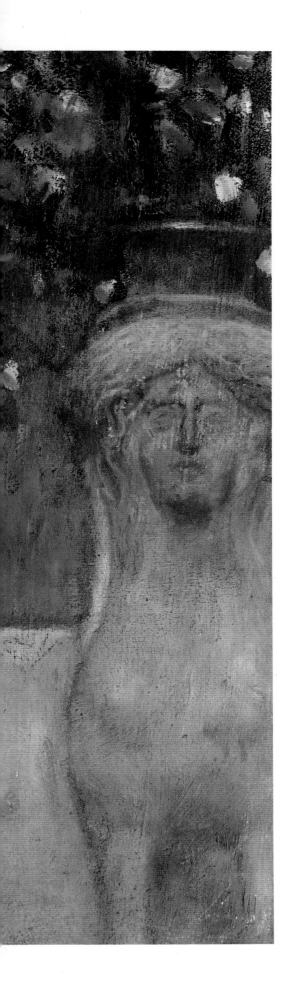

Music I, 1895

Oil on canvas
14½×17½ inches (37×44.5cm)
Bayerische Staatsgemäldesammlungen,
Neue Pinakothek, Munich

Although Klimt's artistic style was already undergoing change, what still remains in his work is a love of sumptuous scenes and allegorical figures. *Music* is one of Klimt's earliest works to make use of gold in order to pay tribute to the art of the past and to give value to that of the present. For Klimt, the painting itself was a material object as well as a method of representation and a transmitter of symbolic meaning. As well as being poised between the fine arts and the crafts, the painting style here hovers between an 'impressionism' in the figure of the girl and the abstract in the flatness of the golden lyre.

A second 'version' of this painting, *Music* (1898), destroyed by fire in 1945, was commissioned by Nikolaus Dumba as one of two sopraporte decorations for his music room. One painting depicted the figure of music in historical terms (Schubert, page 42), the other allegorically.

The motif of the lyre-playing girl was to reappear in two further variations: firstly in *Music*, a color lithograph in the Secession magazine *Ver Sacrum IV* (Sacred Spring) in 1901, and secondly in the figure of 'Poetry' in the *Beethoven Frieze* of 1902.

Throughout his career, even in his landscape paintings, Klimt would produce numerous variations on themes or *leitmotifs*.

Tragedy, 1897

Black chalk, pencil and wash with white
and gold highlights on paper
$16\frac{1}{2} \times 12\frac{1}{2}$ inches (41.9×30.8cm)
Historisches Museum der Stadt Wien,
Vienna

In 1881 Klimt was first asked by the publisher Martin Gerlach to supply designs for his publication *Allegories and Emblems*, a series of pattern books for use in schools, workshops and studios that was to popularise allegorical motifs.

A second series followed between 1895 and 1897, but the educational aims were abandoned in favor of more personal tastes and styles, although the allegories were still largely drawn from ancient historical and mythological sources. Klimt's *Tragedy* appeared on folio 66 in the second portfolio published by Gerlach and his associate Schenk, and discernible in the work are influences from the English Pre-Raphaelite Brotherhood and the Dutch and Belgian Symbolists.

Here the figure of Melpomene has lowered her mask of tragedy (ordinarily symbolizing the inner characteristics normally hidden by the outward personality) to reveal an equally mask-like face. The expression in her eyes is particularly reminiscent of that seen in Khnopff's portraits of his sister Marguerite.

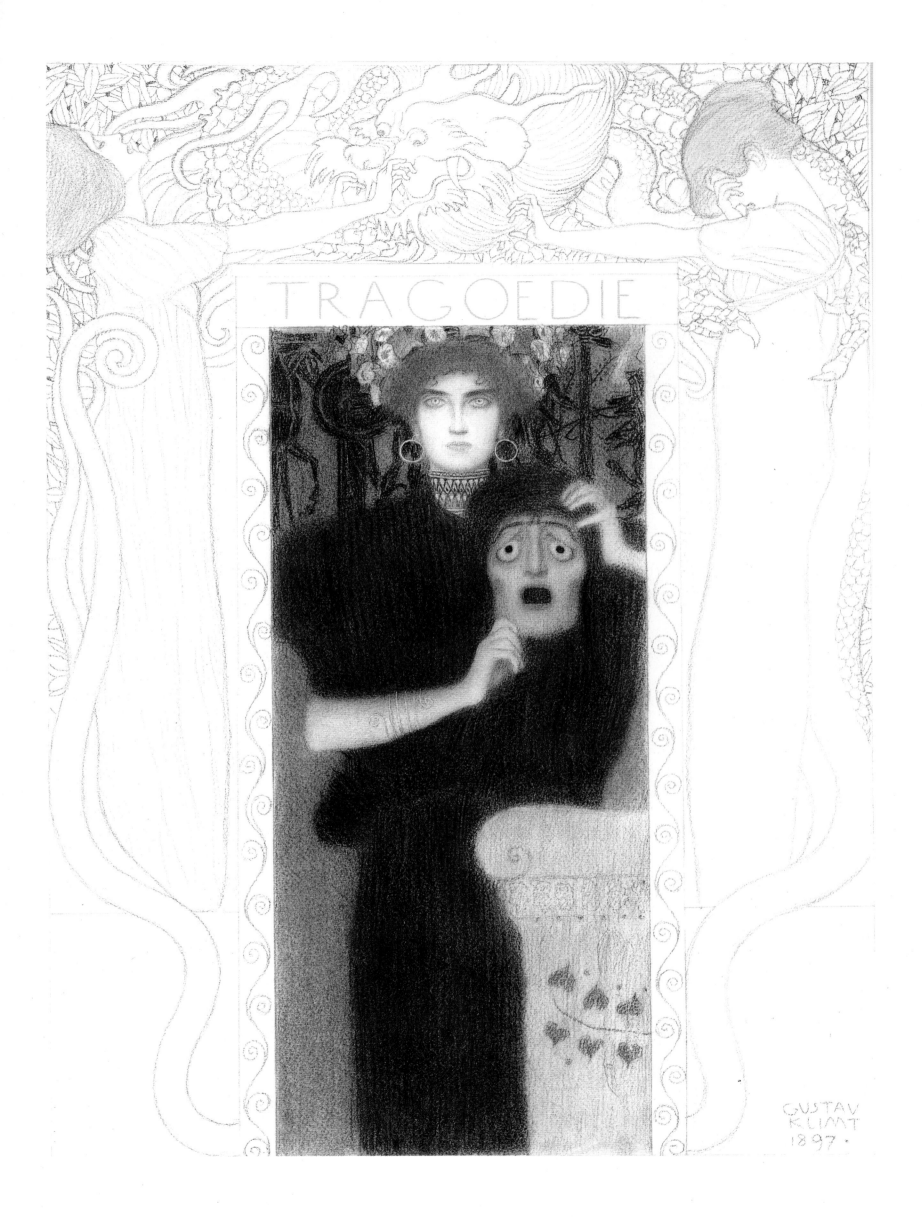

TRAGOEDIE

GUSTAV
KLIMT
1897

Portrait of Sonja Knips, 1898

Oil on canvas
57×57 inches (145×145cm)
Österreichische Galerie, Vienna

1898 saw the first full year of activity of the Vienna Secession with the publication of their magazine *Ver Sacrum* and the first exhibition in March, for which Klimt designed the poster depicting Theseus slaying the Minotaur. The *Portrait of Sonja Knips* was shown at the second Secession exhibition in November 1898, side by side with Klimt's *Pallas Athene* (page 39). In contrast to the frontality and emphasis on surface patterns in *Pallas Athene* which shows the influence of Jugendstil painting, the *Portrait of Sonja Knips* is a painting which appears as gently impressionistic and is the first of Klimt's large, square-format female portraits.

Here the Viennese society belle sits in her garden chair. Behind her head are flowers while in her hand she holds one of Klimt's lost notebooks. The artist had his model hold this in order to create the tense atmosphere of a young woman who has just received some news. The serenity of the mood is broken further by Sonja's hand clasped against the arm of her chair.

At first sight, the *Portrait of Sonja Knips* may bear little relation to the later portraits where increasingly the sitter's clothes are translated into flatter, decorative patterns. However, in the portraits of *Adèle Bloch-Bauer I* (1907, page 71) and *Fritza Riedler* (1906, page 67), a similar off-center triangular structure of Sonja Knips's pose reappears, as well as that certain tension, expressed again through clasped hands.

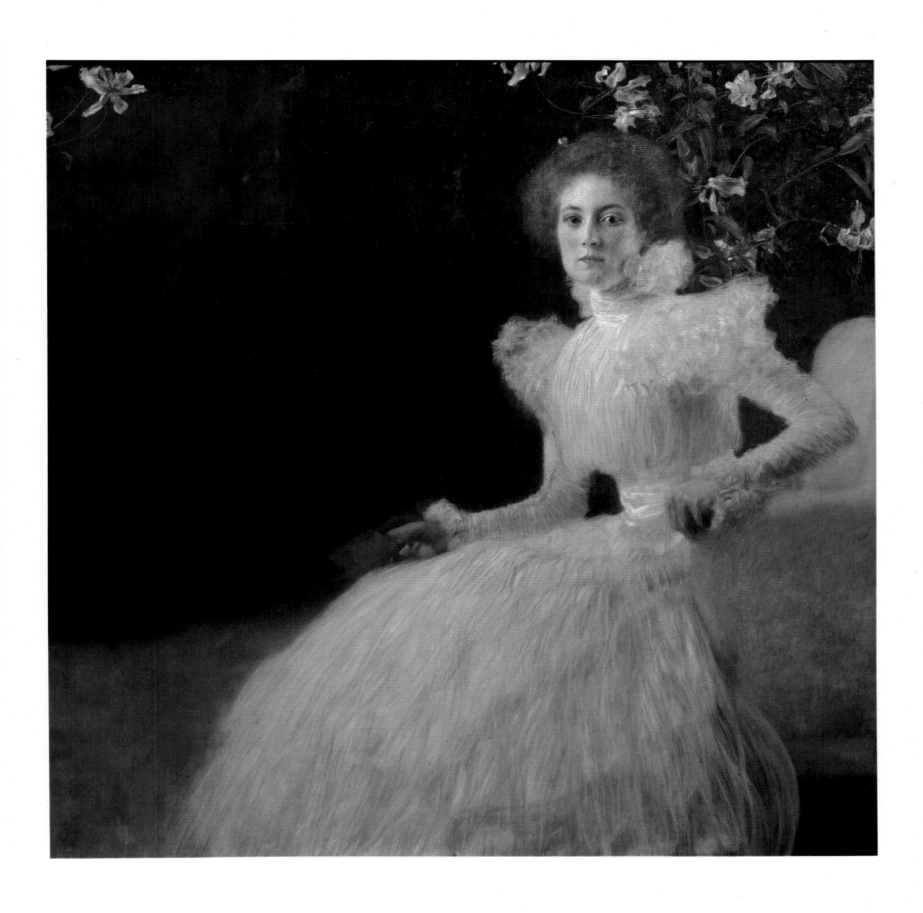

Pallas Athene, 1898

Oil on canvas
29½×29½ inches (75×75cm)
Historisches Museum der Stadt Wien,
Vienna

In 1892 Franz von Stuck had chosen the figure of Athene to be the symbol of the Munich Secession. Now, formally associated with the artists' group, Klimt chose the figure of Athene to stand for his own Vienna Secession, firstly in his poster of Theseus slaying the Minotaur with Athene depicted in profile armed with a spear and shield bearing the gorgon's head. In a square oil painting done the same year and exhibited at the second Secessionist exhibition, Klimt again portrayed Pallas Athene, the warrior Goddess of wisdom, but this time frontally. On her breastplate is the image of the gorgon's head, this time sticking its tongue out at the enemies of the avant-garde.

Pallas Athene is notable not only on account of the beautiful metal frame designed by the artist and made by his sculptor brother Georg, but also in the tiny nude female figure of Nike (Victory) with outstretched arms whose feet rest on an orb held by Athene.

Pallas Athene is, furthermore, another example of Klimt's reworking of a leitmotif. He painted three versions of Athene: firstly in the spandrels of the Kunsthistorisches Museum; secondly, as the more stylized and abstracted figure in the Secession poster; and here, as a triumphant symbol of victory.

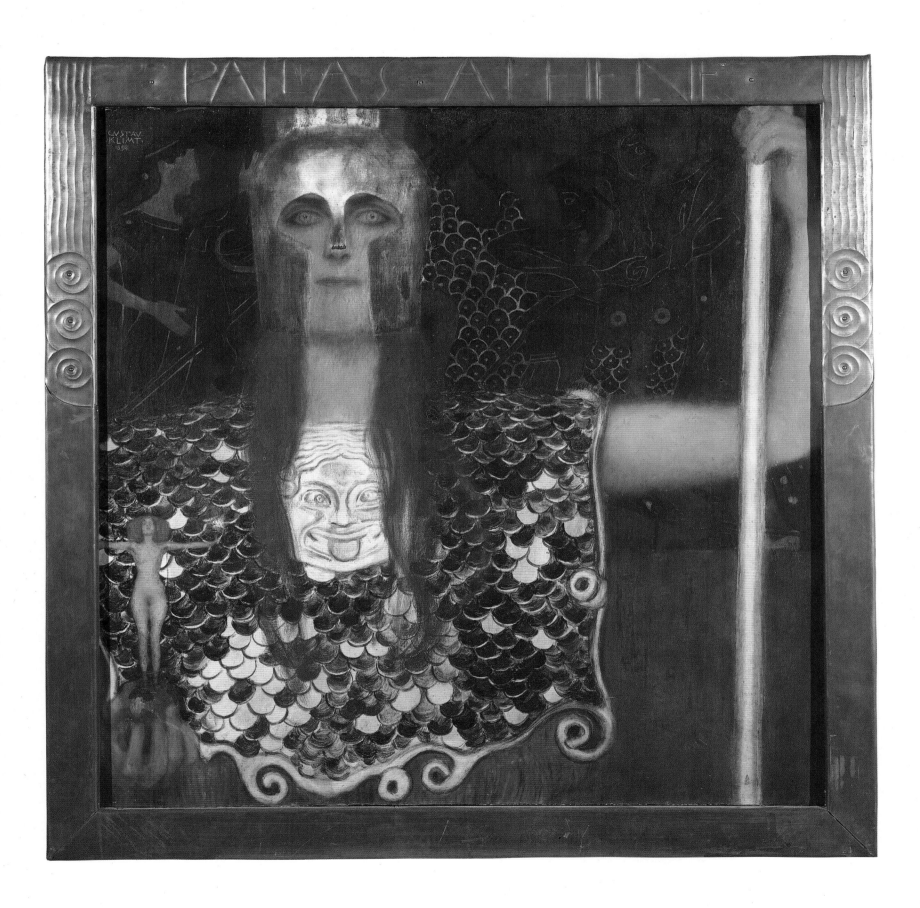

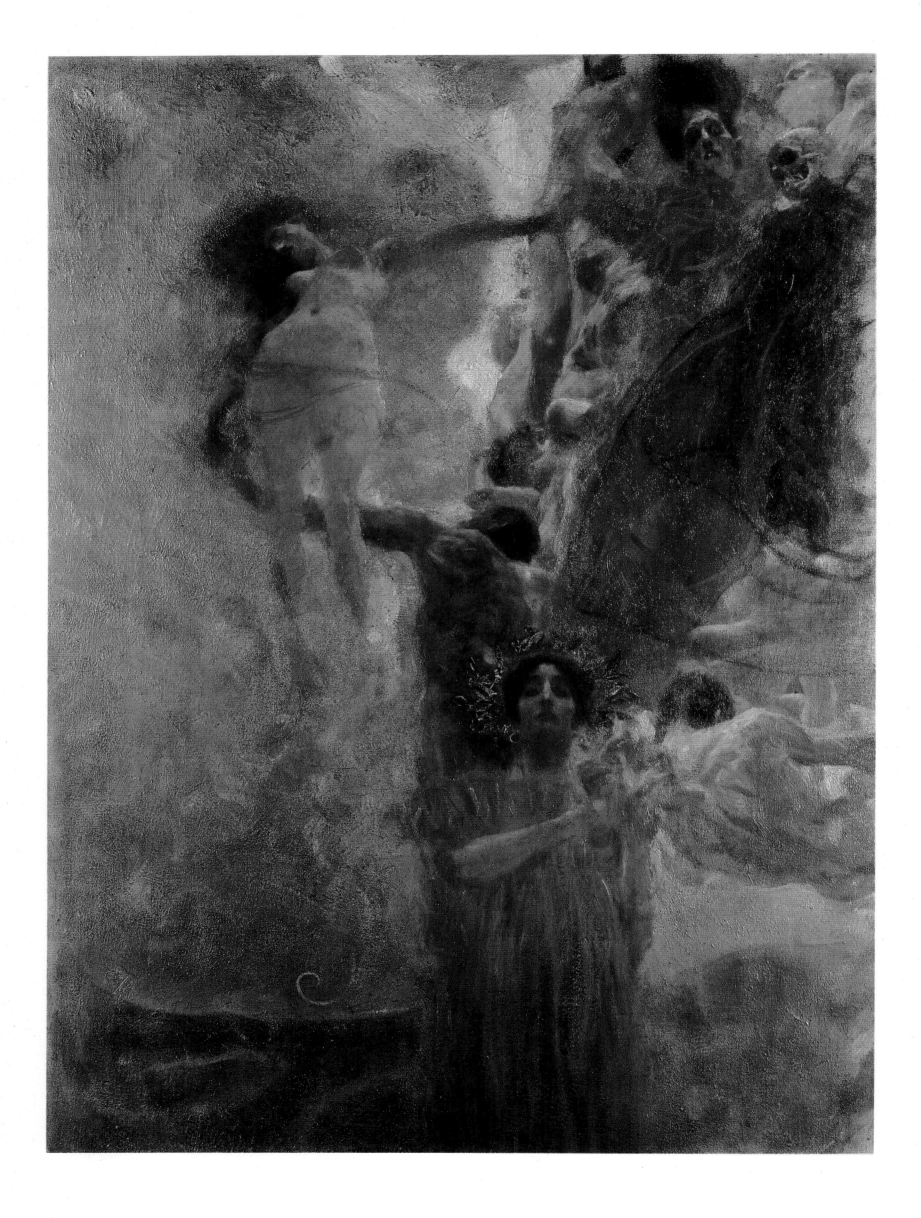

Medicine, 1897-98

Compositional sketch
Oil on canvas
$28\frac{1}{3} \times 21\frac{5}{8}$ inches (72×55cm)
Private collection, Vienna

In 1891 the Arts Commission of Vienna University submitted plans for the decoration of the ceiling of the Great Hall, the Aula of Heinrich von Ferstel's university building. The plan was to adorn the ceiling with representations of the four faculties of the University – Theology, Philosophy, Medicine and Jurisprudence. Having dismissed the idea of an open competition, in 1893 the Commission invited Franz Matsch to submit an overall plan and proposed that he and Klimt, who had successfully collaborated on large-scale works previously, should produce a study for the central ceiling panel on the theme of *The Victory of Light over Darkness.* The ceiling panel and the panel representing Theology were to be produced by Matsch, while Klimt undertook the remaining three panels and ten lunette paintings. Although there were criticisms of the initial sketches, work on the panels went ahead. When the first of Klimt's university paintings, *Philosophy,* was exhibited in 1900, it was obvious that he was traveling on a completely different artistic course from the one that originally secured the commission, and it unleashed a fury of protests from both the public and the press.

When the second painting, *Medicine,* was exhibited in 1901, Klimt had fully refined the elements within the compositional sketch. The chain of figures in the finished painting lost its *sfumato* effect to become clearly defined bodies of men and women in the various stages of development from infancy to old age and death. The floating female figure, which would become the object of fierce criticism, was further refined to display pubic hair and floats above a figure in a foetal position. At the base of the painting the figure of Hygieia bears the healing powers of medicine.

On 19 March 1901 the Imperial Public Prosecutor's office applied for a permit allowing the confiscation of the edition of *Ver Sacrum* which contained the sketch of *Medicine* on the grounds that it was pornographic. Two days later, however, the application was rejected by the Criminal Bench of the Imperial Provincial Court which did not distinguish between the tradition of nude painting in Europe and Klimt's art.

Nuda Veritas, 1899

Oil on canvas
$99\frac{1}{4} \times 22\frac{1}{8}$ inches (252×6.2cm)
Bild-Archiv der Österreichischen Nationalbibliothek, Vienna

The fourth exhibition of the Secession in March 1899 showed a mixture of works by the Austrian members and their contemporaries abroad. At this exhibition Klimt showed his *Schubert at the Piano* and *Nuda Veritas* in which he experimented with the pointillist technique of painting using spots of color laid side by side that blended not on the canvas, but in the spectator's eye.

Nuda Veritas was bought by Hermann Bahr, a literary adviser to *Ver Sacrum* and author of a collection of essays *On Criticism of Modernity* in which he preached the end of naturalism, and *The Overcoming of Naturalism* in which he defined a new psychology, idealism and romanticism, that would compensate for naturalism. Bahr declared that the artist should be freed from creating reflections of reality in order to create lyrical expressions.

The quote from Schiller at the top of *Nuda Veritas* reinforces the problems that this new approach to art would face:

If by your actions and by your art you cannot please everyone – please a few. To please everyone is bad. Schiller. Naked Truth.

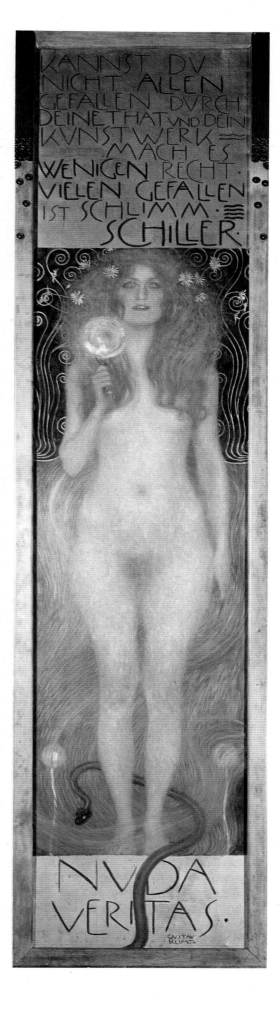

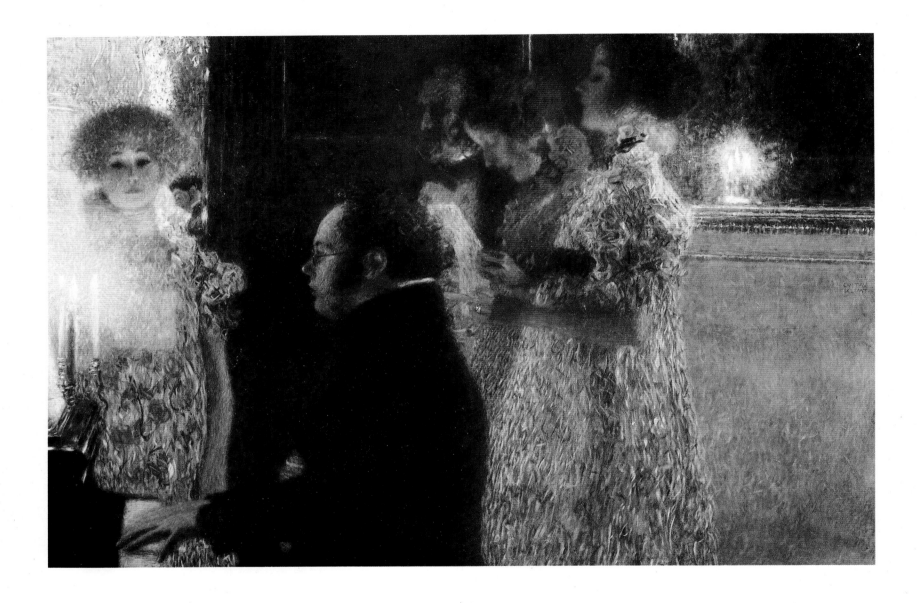

Schubert at the Piano, 1899

Oil on canvas
59×78¾ inches (150×200cm)
Destroyed 1945

To accompany the two sopraporte representations of Music produced for Nikolaus Dumba's music room, Klimt painted *Schubert at the Piano* which was displayed at the fourth Secession exhibition in March 1899, prior to installation at the Palais Dumba. In contrast to the *Pallas Athene*, Klimt's picture showing the Viennese composer Franz Peter Schubert (1797-1828) brought him considerable success, and once again the debt to the Post-Impressionists is apparent in the loose pointillist technique.

In 1916 an operetta called *Das Dreimädlerhaus* (The House of Three Maidens) by Heinrich Berte and R H Bartsch was performed. The story was woven around Schubert's life and un-happy love for Hannerl Tscholl, the youngest of a glazier's three daughters. *Schwammel* (mushroom), as Schubert was nicknamed, is depicted as a short, stocky, bespectacled musician who was too shy and awkward to win the love of the girl he wished to marry.

Whether in *Schubert at the Piano* Klimt is offering us a similar view of the composer's life – could the young girl beside the piano be Hannerl, while her sisters and father stand behind the composer – we can only speculate. It seems more likely, though less romantic, that the painting depicts Schubert as the music tutor to the three daughters of Count Esterhazy at Zseliz where he was employed in 1818 and 1824.

42

Portrait of Serena Lederer,

1899

Oil on canvas
74×32⅝ inches (188×83cm)
Österreichische Galerie, Vienna

On many occasions Klimt's art has been
called an expression of the sensuality that,
although hidden by social conventions,
was prevalent in Viennese society. Most
of the sitters for Klimt's portraits were the
wives and daughters of wealthy men; they
were themselves knowledgable art lovers
and their patronage played an important
role in the cultural flowering of the
period. Although already an established
painter, Klimt no doubt found his entry
into the cultured bourgeois circles of
Viennese salons eased by his brother
Ernst's marriage to Helen Flöge, one of
three daughters of a wealthy industrialist.

The *Portrait of Serena Lederer* depicts
the wife of August Lederer, her dark eyes
and hair standing out against the pearly
whiteness of her dress which, in some
areas, 'fuses' with the background.

In addition to accumulating the great-
est collection of Klimt's work in private
ownership (including *Philosophy* and the
Beethoven Frieze), August Lederer was
the main financier and co-founder of the
Wiener Werkstätte. For the portrait of his
wife, Lederer paid Klimt 35,000 crowns
and subsequently lent him a further
30,000 crowns to enable Klimt to buy
back his three paintings for the University's Great Hall decoration scheme.

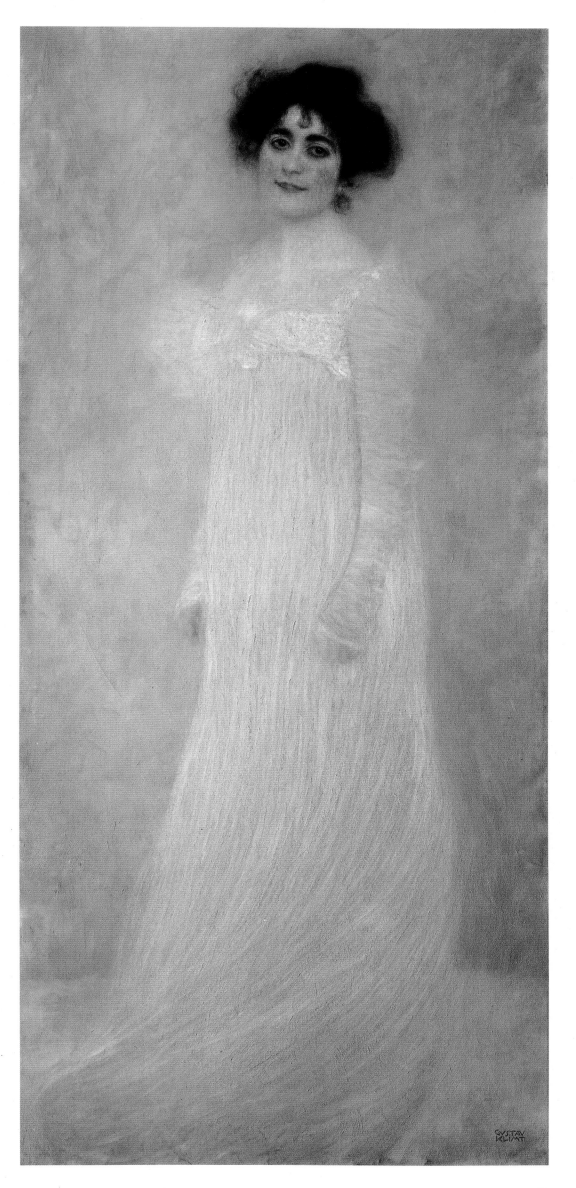

Hygieia (detail from Medicine),

1900-1907

Oil on canvas

169¼×118⅓ inches (430×300cm; whole painting)

Destroyed 1945

The three canvasses for the University of Vienna's Great Hall, *Philosophy, Jurisprudence* and *Medicine* (of which *Hygieia* is a detail), were owned by Klimt after he had bought back the commission from the University, but later he re-sold them to August Lederer and Ditha Moser. Eventually all three paintings were acquired by the Österreichische Galerie in Vienna. These, along with other important works, were stored at the Schloss Immendorf in Niederösterreich, but were destroyed after retreating SS troops set the castle alight to prevent it falling to the Allied forces in the final days of World War II. Apart from black and white photographs of the completed paintings and the oils sketches, the detail of *Medicine* showing Hygieia survives only in color reproductions.

Ernst Stohr wrote in *Ver Sacrum*, IV (1901):

Between Birth and Death, Life plays itself out, and Life itself, on its way from the cradle to the grave, brings with it that profound suffering for which Hygieia, the miracle-working daughter of Aesculapius, has found the mild and healing salve.

But not everyone had the same response to the painting: many considered it an affront to good taste and unsuitable for the intended position in the University, while others again accused Klimt of painting pornography.

Looking at *Hygieia*, it is possible to see how Klimt's approach to painting had changed from the impressionistic approach in *Sonja Knips* (page 37) or *Serena Lederer* (page 43) to a more decorative, two-dimensional manner.

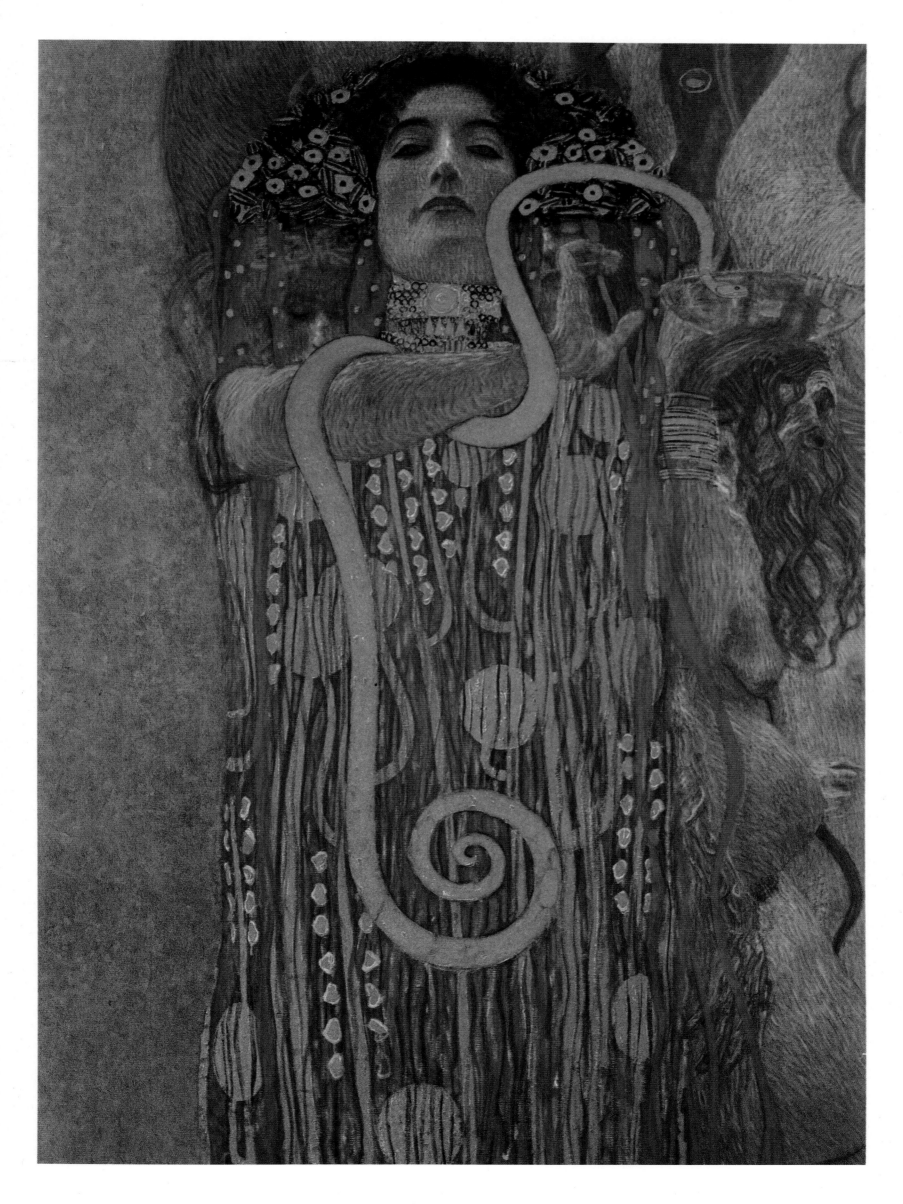

Island in the Attersee, c. 1901

Oil on canvas
39⅜×39⅜ inches (100×100cm)
Private collection, courtesy Galerie St
Etienne, New York

Of the 230 pictures Klimt painted, at least 54 were landscapes. Yet among the several thousand drawings he made for his portraits and allegorical compositions, only three sketches for landscapes exist. Furthermore, Klimt also began painting landscapes at a late stage in his career: his first landscapes date from around 1898, by which time he was 36 years old.

During 1900 and 1901, Klimt took the Attersee as his subject and produced several variations, including the nearly identical pair of paintings *On the Attersee I* and *II*. All, however, have the square format that he had been using since 1898 and a raised horizon.

In *Island in the Attersee* the island appears in the distance at the top right corner of the picture. In the remaining area, Klimt concentrates on the treatment of the water's surface. Although Klimt was familiar with the techniques of the Impressionist and Pointillist painters, he was not ultimately concerned with the physical appearance of objects but with understanding the essence of things behind appearances and, as such, created 'mood' paintings. In this picture, in the treatment of the surface of the lake, Klimt does not introduce any element that might disturb the eye and halt the viewer in his or her contemplation of nature.

Goldfish, 1901-02

Oil on canvas
59×18⅛ inches (150×46cm)
Private collection, Solothurn
Courtesy Galerie Wetz, Salzburg

Around the time that Klimt was painting *Goldfish* he was also working on several landscape subjects that had water as an important compositional element (*The Swamp*, 1900; *Island on the Attersee* c. 1901; *On the Attersee I* and *II*, 1900). The leitmotif of water was one that was also shared by writers and artists of the Symbolist movement (Debussy's *La Mer*; André Gide's *Paludes* and Arnold Böcklin's *The Calm Sea*). In ancient Greece, water had been seen as the essentially feminine element, the source of all potentialities in existence, the liquid counterpart of light and the source and grave of all things in the universe. Because water was also equated with the continual flux of the manifest world and with the unconscious, it had the power to dissolve, purify and regenerate.

Not only in his landscapes, but in *Goldfish* and even *Medicine*, the life-giving force of water became Klimt's metaphor for the subjective world. Gold was used increasingly in Klimt's work, sometimes as a background color, in other instances in a structural role to represent forms and space, such as here in *Goldfish*.

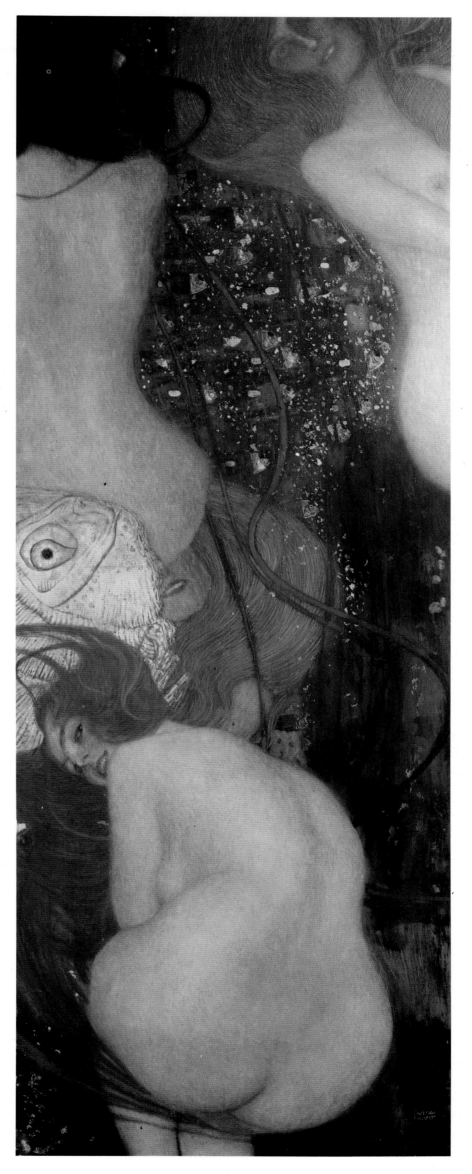

Portrait of Emilie Flöge, 1902

Oil on canvas
71¼×33 inches (181×84cm)
Historisches Museum der Stadt Wien,
Vienna

Emilie Flöge was Klimt's sister-in-law
(his brother Ernst married Helen Flöge)
and lifelong companion: it was Emilie
that Klimt called for after he suffered his
disabling stroke. With her sisters, Emilie
ran a leading Viennese fashion salon, the
Casa Piccolo, in premises designed by the
Wiener Werkstätte. As well as painting
Emilie's portrait, Klimt also designed textiles, dresses and even labels for garments
for her. Emilie had also collected an im-
pressive selection of lace and textiles from
eastern Europe and incorporated ethnic
motifs into her designs. But more import-
antly, her work represented the way
fashion, like all the applied arts, was
becoming part of the avant-garde's desire
for reforms in art, design and life. Compared to Sonja Knips' tightly waisted
dress, Emilie Flöge's 'rational' dress, as it
was called, permitted a greater degree of
natural movement.

In Klimt's portrait we see the beginnings of the so-called 'golden style' in his
art: on the linear designs of Emilie's dress
are scattered reflective motifs in a flatter,
more geometrical style. The distinguish-
ing characteristic of Klimt's later portraiture, this creation of abstract patterns
while retaining a naturalistic rendering
for the faces and hands, emerges first in
the *Portrait of Emilie Flöge.*

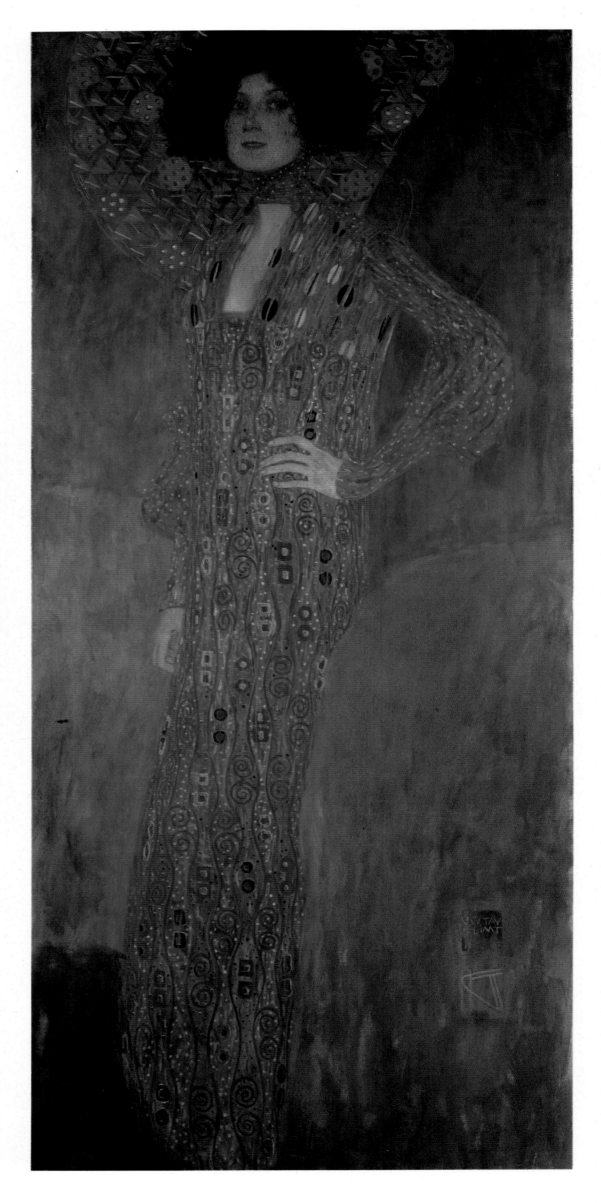

48

Beech Wood I, c. 1902

Oil on canvas
39⅜×39⅜ inches (100×100cm)
Moderne Galerie, Dresden

One of Klimt's main artistic influences was the Swiss painter Ferdinand Hodler (1853-1918). Not only was Klimt to paraphrase Hodler's angels from *The Chosen One* for his own chorus of heavenly angels in the *Beethoven Frieze* (pages 56-7), but also in *Beech Wood I*, he followed Hodler's theory of 'parallelism' whereby the repetition of objects increased the visual and decorative effects. In *Beech Wood I* Klimt arranged in a rhythmical sequence an unending repetition of tree trunks.

Once again Klimt produced a series of variations on the theme of the interior of forests: *Forest of Firs I* and *II* from 1901, *The Birchwood,* c. 1903 and two variations of the beech wood, first in 1902 and again in 1903. By the time Klimt was painting *Beech Wood I*, his treatment had changed from the soft-focus all-over view of the forest to one where each tree trunk is a separate, individual organic entity. The forest interior for Klimt is like water, both tranquil and full of life as well as 'infinite.'

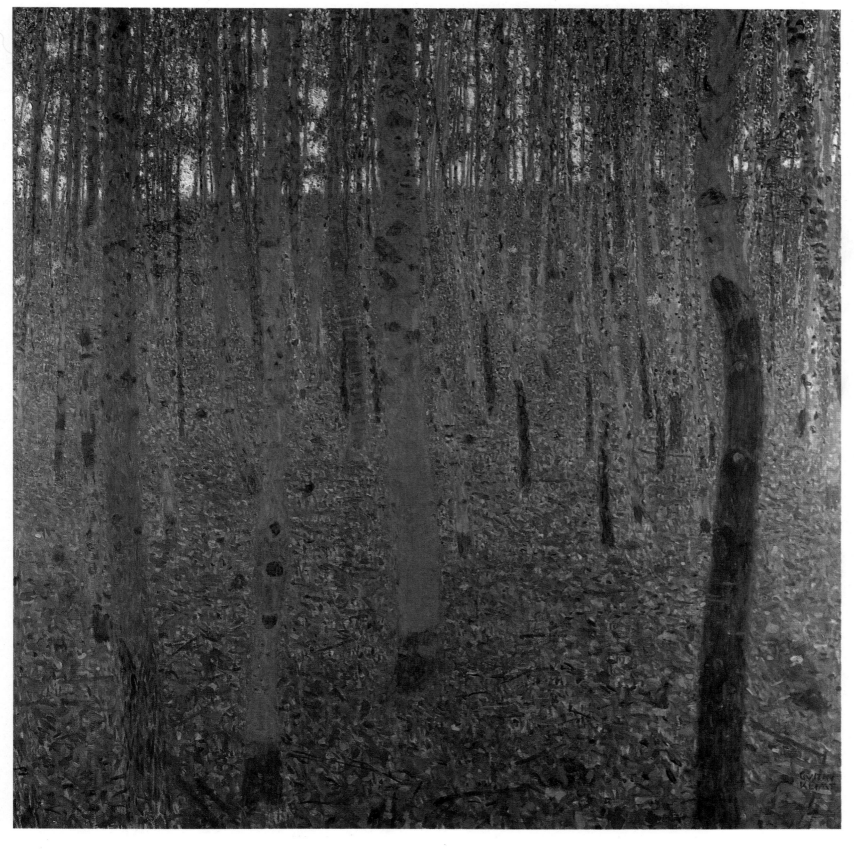

Hope I, 1903

Oil on canvas
74½×26⅜ inches (189.2×67cm)
National Gallery of Canada, Ottawa

Although painted in 1903, *Hope I* was not shown publicly until the International Kunstschau in 1909, the first of two finished paintings on the theme of the pregnant woman and one of the most personal of all Klimt's works. It eventually became part of the private collection of Fritz Warndorfer, co-founder of the Wiener Werkstätte, who kept it behind locked doors in a specially constructed 'shrine.'

The 'hope' of the title, personified by the pregnant woman, is ambiguous: what should be a tender painting is, like the earlier *Love* (1895), an expression of 'angst.' Behind the expectant mother lurk the faces and masks of decay and death, presaging evil and not good; 'angst' at a time of happiness. While her hands rest on her body protecting her unborn child, the woman looks out at the spectator, her eyes curiously wide. Here, the woman's body is again rendered naturalistically while the background is compressed into a shallow space and treated decoratively.

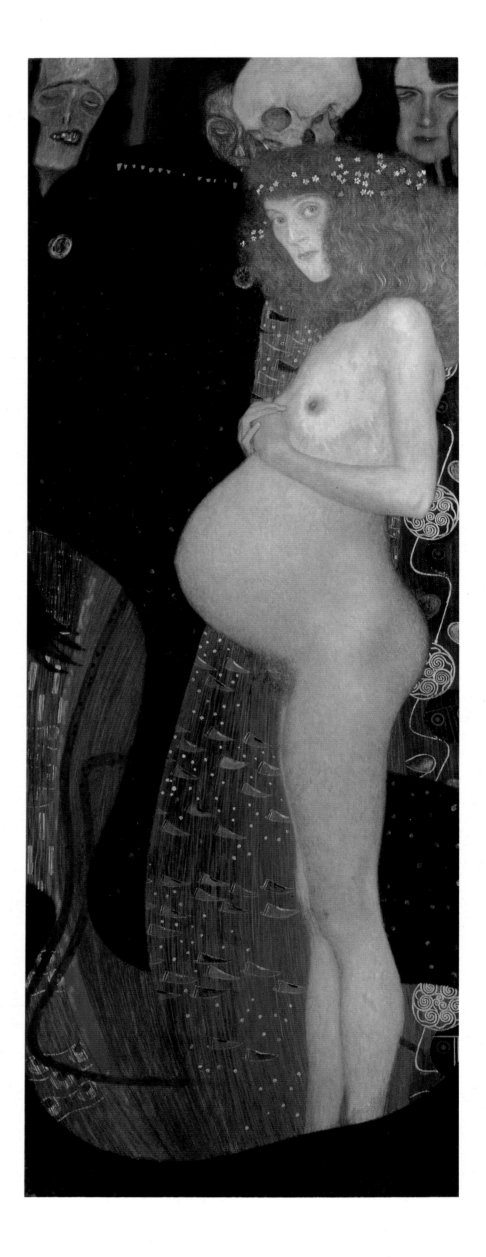

Water Snakes (Friends) I,

c. 1904-07

Mixed media on parchment
$19^{11}/_{16} \times 7^{7}/_{8}$ inches (50×20cm)
Österreichische Galerie, Vienna

Water Snakes I demonstrates Klimt's ability to combine a powerful specific naturalism and an expressive distortion of forms in the treatment of the two bodies with an elaborate surface decoration suggestive of space and depth. The two bodies are overlapped and partially covered by flowing hair, allowing us to see only two arms and one head. We cannot visually disengage one body from the other in the illusion of fluid, almost boneless, underwater existence. In 1904, it is generally assumed, Klimt began regularly making nude drawings of several professional models who were often present simultaneously in his studio.

On one level, *Water Snakes I* can be interpreted as an expression of lesbian love – as Klimt, like many contemporary writers and artists, was concerned with expressing and championing female sexuality. On another level, since by tradition water serpents are hermaphroditic creatures, and in keeping with the mood of Klimt's other 'water' inspired works, it may signify primordial instinctual nature, the uncontrolled upsurging of the life force. *Water Snakes I* was the first of two explorations of this theme. A second version was painted during the same years, though the more general theme of female friendship was to continue throughout his work.

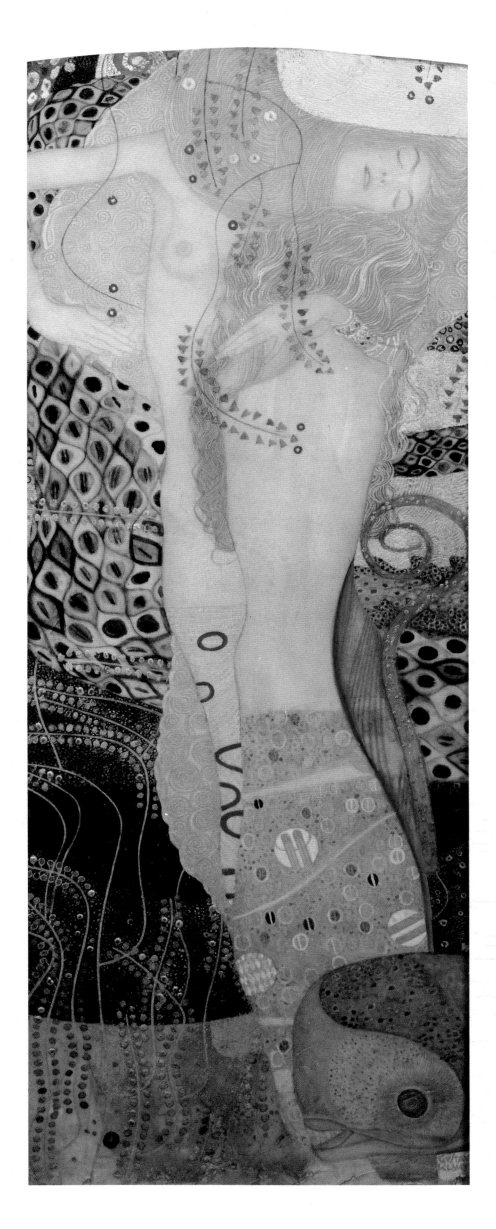

Judith I, 1901

Oil on canvas
33×16½ inches (84×42cm)
Österreichische Galerie, Vienna

In *Judith I* Klimt retained the frontal presentation of the figure that appears in *Pallas Athene* (page 39) for his interpretation and depiction of the liberating Jewess who killed Nebuchadnezzar's captain Holofernes.

Against the background of golden trees, Judith is depicted in a gold collar and girdle, a thin cloth draped over her shoulders reveals one breast, with half-closed eyes and parted lips. In her hand, only half visible, is the head of Holofernes.

But Klimt has not portrayed Judith as the heroine who killed in order to free her people from the Assyrians, but as a sensuous woman, whose lust has turned her into a seductress and murderer.

Although *Judith I* has 'Judith and Holofernes' embossed on the metal frame, the picture was often referred to, even in Klimt's own lifetime, as *Salome.* It is important to remember that Salome caused the death of John the Baptist, while Judith killed Holofernes with her own hand. This allegorical rendering of revenge, which is visible also in the *Hostile Powers* of the *Beethoven Frieze* is in part derived from the popular subject of the femme fatale at the turn of the century and partly from the change in women's position in society, which was viewed by many as a threat to the status quo.

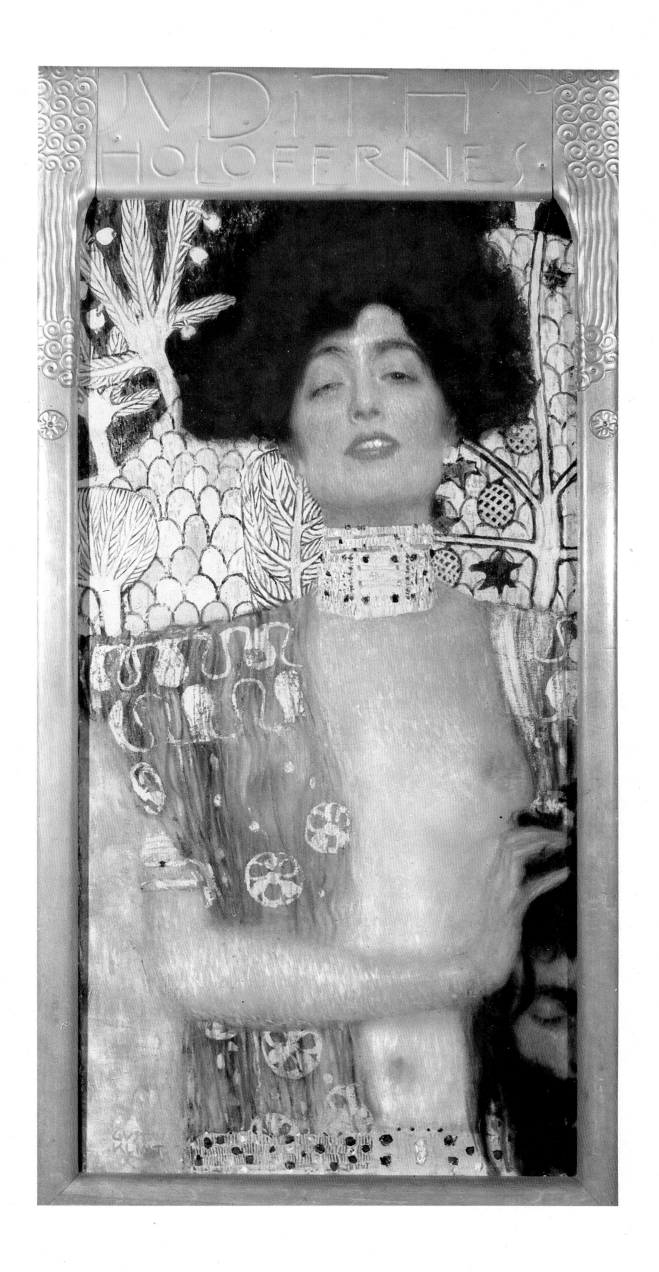

The Beethoven Frieze

The 14th exhibition of the Secession from April to June 1902 centered on a single work, Max Klinger's monumental polychrome sculpture of Beethoven (page 000), while other works were executed to form a background to it. In the long room to the left of the main entrance of the Secession building, Klimt produced the *Beethoven Frieze*, an enormous composition lining three walls with six plaster panels painted in casein colors and decorated with gold and semi-precious stones. Unlike many of the other 'supporting' works on display, which were destroyed after the exhibition, the *Beethoven Frieze* became part of the Lederer collection in 1915 and was eventually acquired for the Austrian nation in 1972.

The three painted walls formed a coherent sequence. On the first long wall opposite the entrance was depicted the theme of 'longing for happiness' personified by three figures (*The Sufferings of Weak Humanity*) who beseech the knight in armor (*The Well-Armed Strong One*), behind whom stand the figures of Compassion and Ambition who urge the knight to struggle for happiness.

On the narrow wall were depicted the *Hostile Powers*: the giant Typhon and his three Gorgon daughters with golden serpents entwined in their hair; behind them, Sickness, Mania and Death; on the right, Debauchery, Unchastity and Excess, and far right, Corroding Grief. Above them fly the longings and desires of mankind.

On the second long wall, the 'longing for happiness' finds solace in Poetry (a figure similar to the one already seen in *Music I*). 'The Arts' (in an arrangement similar to the chain of human life in *Philosophy* and *Medicine*) lead into the Kingdom of the Ideal with the Choir of Heavenly Angels surrounding an embracing couple representing *This Kiss for the Whole World*.

It is possible to interpret the *Beethoven Frieze*, especially the last panel, as a visual paraphrase of the emotions and ideals expressed by Beethoven in the final movement of the Ninth Symphony, in which Beethoven set to music Schiller's *Ode to Joy*, and from which Klimt borrowed the phrase: 'Diesen Kuss der ganzen Welt.'

Below:
Hostile Forces, 1902
Detail from the *Beethoven Frieze*
Casein paint on plaster
7 ft 2⅛×20 ft 10½ inches (220×636cm)
Österreichische Galerie, Vienna

Right:
Yearning for Happiness, 1902
Detail from the *Beethoven Frieze*
Casein paint on plaster
7 ft 2⅛×45 ft 2½ inches (220×1378cm)
Österreichische Galerie, Vienna

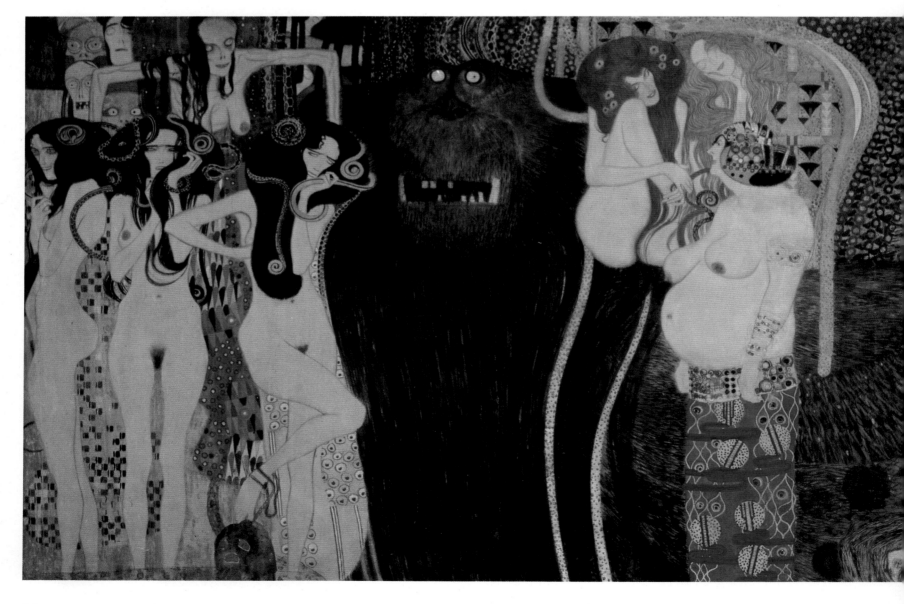

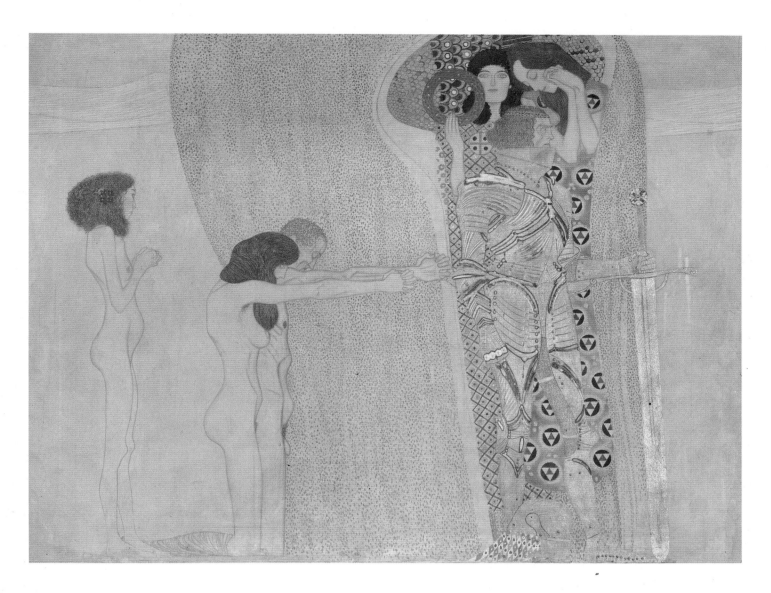

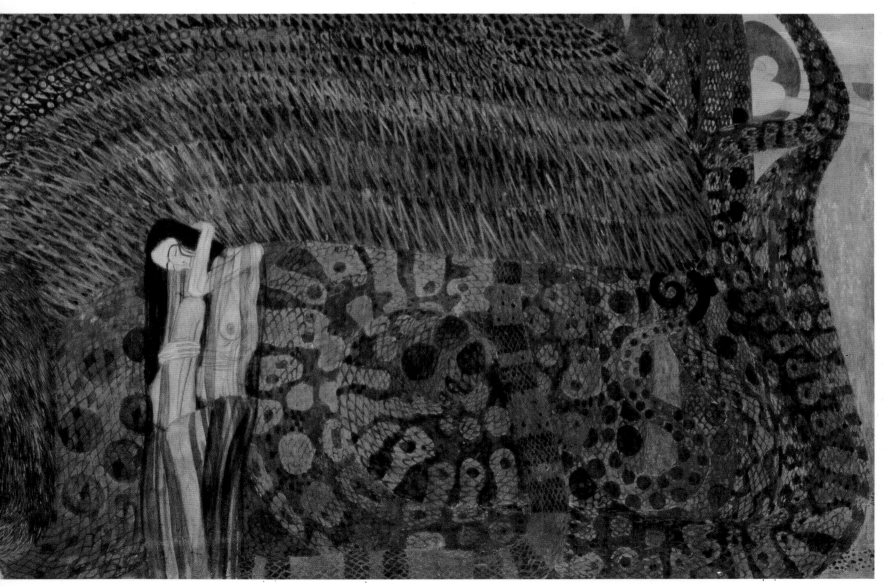

Right and below:
***The Yearning for Happiness
Finds Fulfillment in Poetry,***
1902
Detail from the *Beethoven Frieze*
Casein paint on plaster
7 ft 2⅛×45 ft 4 inches (220×1381cm)
Österreichische Galerie, Vienna

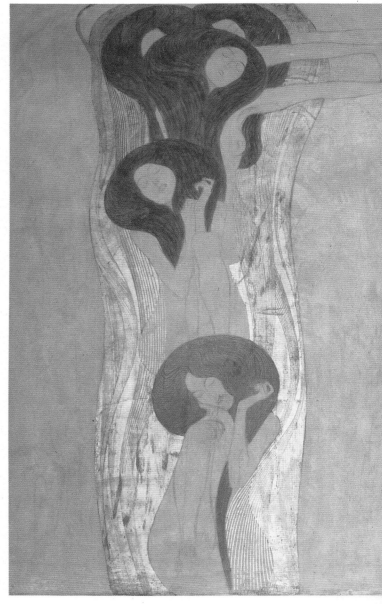

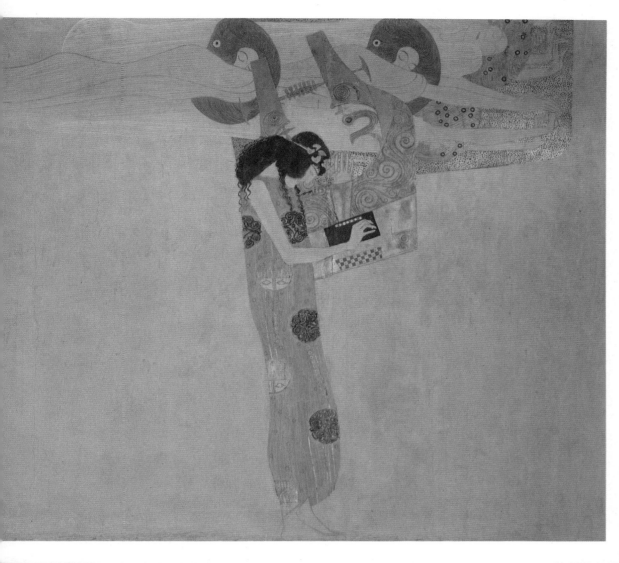

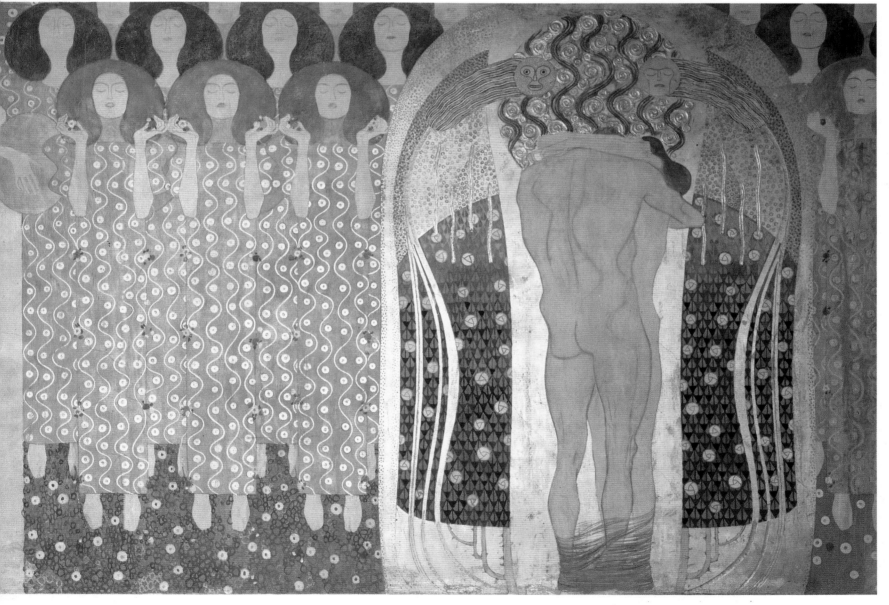

The Stoclet Frieze

The Belgian financier Adolphe Stoclet originally intended to build a villa for himself and his wife in Vienna. When his father died, however, Stoclet returned to Belgium and with his inheritance was able to commission from Josef Hoffmann a suitably grand residence. The monumentality and elegance of the exterior of the Palais Stoclet, clad in glistening white Norwegian marble, was echoed inside with rooms of large proportions where special emphasis was given to the 'public' rooms for entertaining, and much thought given to housing and displaying the Stoclets' collection of Oriental and European art. Many artists within the original Secession and the Wiener Wesk-tätte contributed to the decorations, but by far the most outstanding was the huge mosaic frieze which Klimt designed for the dining room, which was subsequently executed by Leopold Forstner, known simply as the *Stoclet Frieze.*

The frieze was to be made in gold and silver with enamel, coral and semi-precious stones set against a white marble background. On each of the two long walls are seven panels depicting the tree of life. On the end wall there is a tall, thin panel of abstract design. The panels on each wall are identical except for the second panels: on the left-hand wall there is the standing figure of a woman in three-quarter profile who symbolizes Expectation, while opposite her on the right-hand wall is the embracing couple representing Fulfillment. In the penultimate panels on each wall, the coiling branches of the tree of life are set behind the motif of a rose bush (also called the magic bush) with its stylized flowers and thorns.

The *Stoclet Frieze*, Klimt's only true mosaic, fuses together a wide variety of influences. While retaining the naturalistic treatment for the hands and faces of the figures, Klimt drew upon Byzantine mosaics he had seen in Ravenna in 1903, Mycenean ornament in the scroll-like tree of life, and the frontality of Egyptian art in the figure of Expectation.

The treatment of clothing in a two-dimensional decorative manner looks back to the *Portrait of Emilie Flöge* (page 48) and the figure of Hygieia (page 45) in *Medicine,* while the embracing figures of Fulfillment are a reworking of the theme of the embrace already seen in *Love* (page 31) and the *Beethoven Frieze* (pages 54-55), and to be seen again in Klimt's most famous of paintings, *The Kiss* (page 79).

Right:
Expectation, c. 1905-09
Working drawing for the Stoclet Frieze Tempera, watercolor, gold paint, silver bronze, chalk, pencil, white bodycolor, gold and silver leaf on paper.
76×45½ inches (193×115cm)
Österreichisches Museum für Angewandte Kunst, Vienna

Overleaf, left:
Fulfillment, c. 1905-09
Working drawing for the Stoclet Frieze Tempera, watercolor, gold paint, silver bronze, chalk, pencil, white bodycolor, gold and silver leaf on paper.
76×45¼ inches (193×115cm)
Österreichisches Museum für Angewandte Kunst, Vienna

Overleaf, right:
Tree of Life (detai), c. 1905-09
Working drawing for the Stoclet Frieze Tempera, watercolor, gold paint, silver bronze, chalk, pencil, white bodycolor, gold and silver leaf on paper.
76¾×46½ inches (194×115cm)
Österreichisches Museum für Angewandte Kunst, Vienna

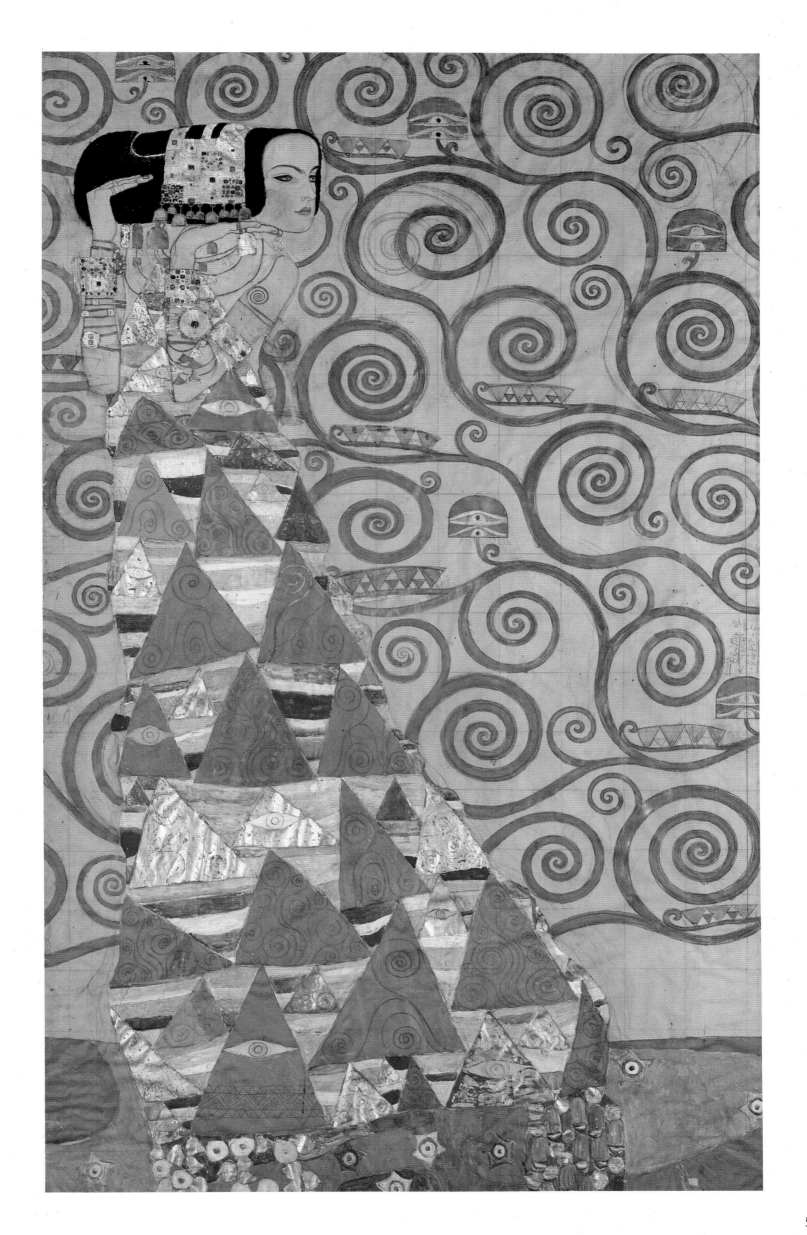

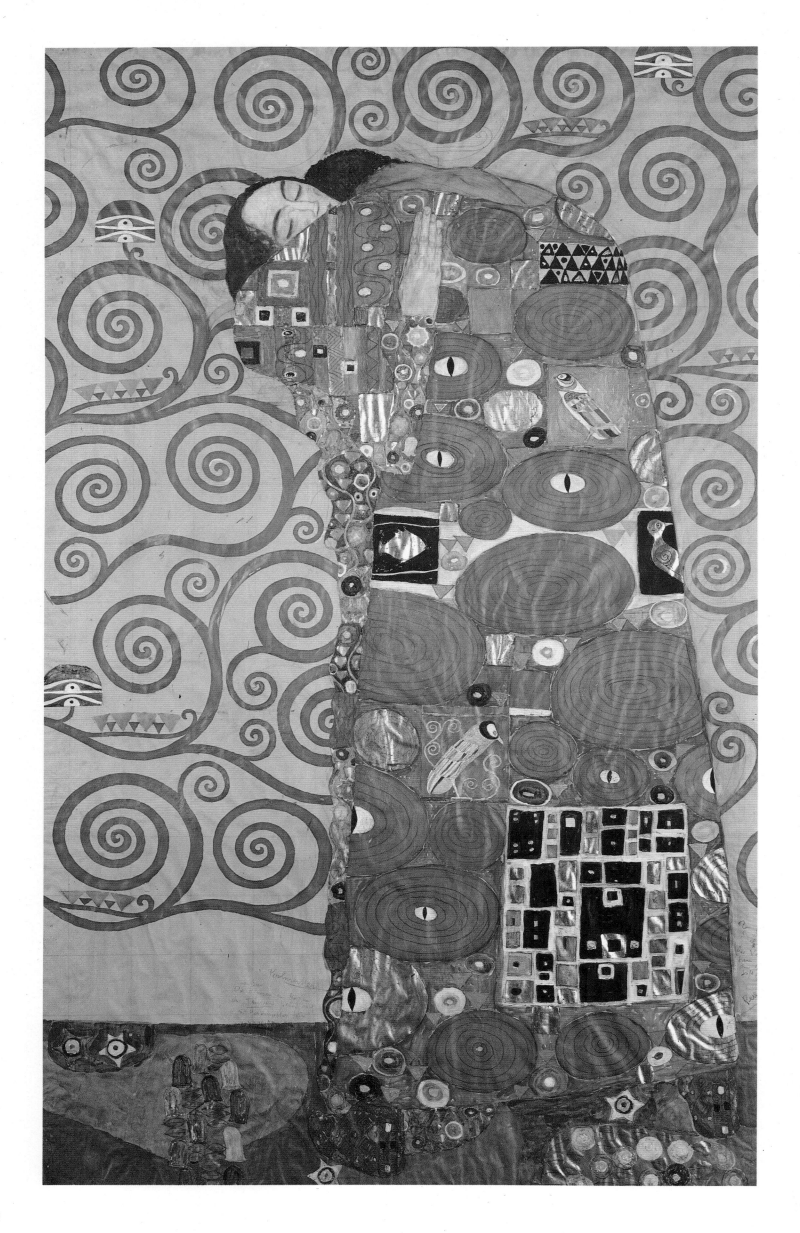

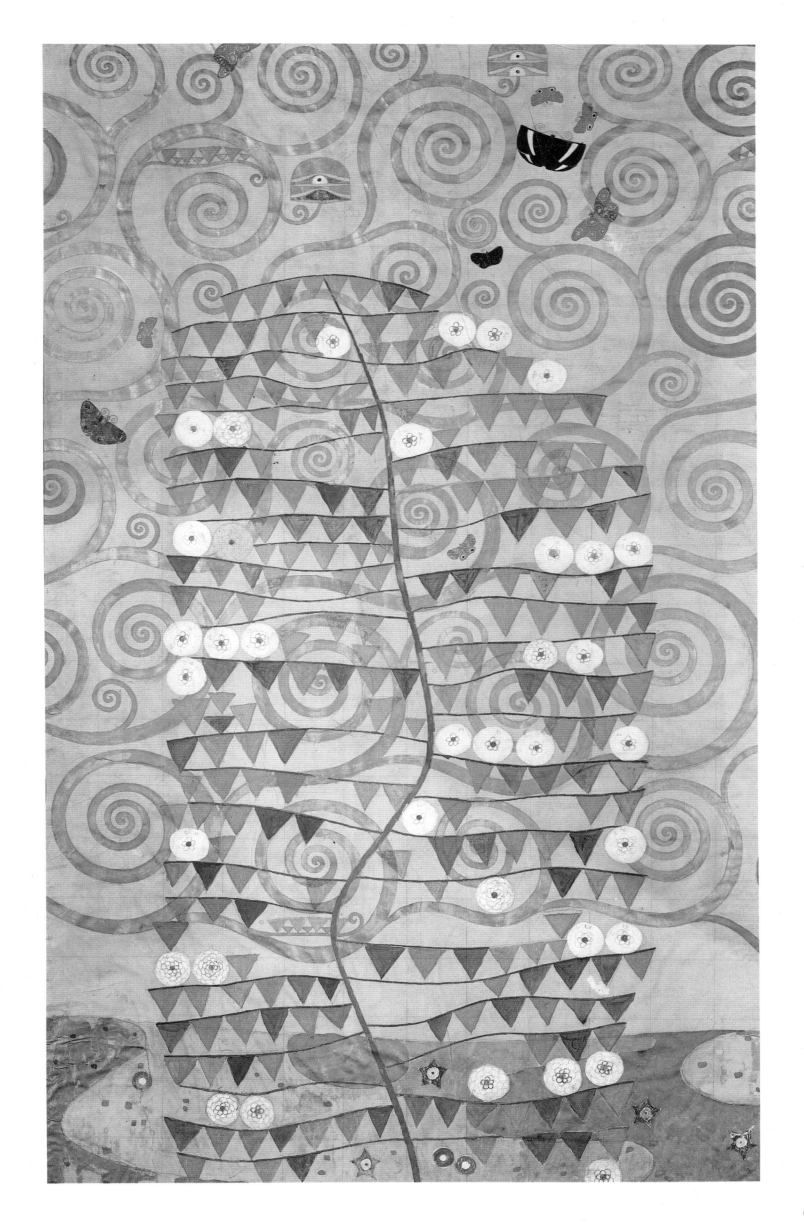

The Three Ages of Woman,

1905
Oil on canvas
70⅞×70⅞ inches (180×180cm)
Galleria Nazionale d'Arte Moderna,
Rome

Exhibited at the Second Exhibition of the Deutscher Künstlerhaus in Berlin, in the *Three Ages of Woman* Klimt deals with the central theme of the cycle of life, a theme already apparent in the *Procession of the Dead* (1903), *Hope I* (1903) and in the university paintings.

In the *Three Ages of Woman* differing degrees of realism are employed to contrast youth and old age: the young woman holding the sleeping child is stylized and becomes part of the background decoration, while the figure of the old woman is treated naturalistically. The contrast between the two has been seen in symbolic terms where youth is characterized by possibilities and change, but old age is marked by unchanging uni-

formity. But yet, as in *Death and Life* (1916), the sleeping youth are unaware of the impending threat of age and decay.

When this painting was exhibited, it was hung alongside *The Kiss* (1907-09) and it is possible that Klimt conceived the two paintings as a diptych. In addition to having the same dimensions, when viewed together the two paintings thematically supplement each other by showing that love leads to procreation; life in its different stages; and that the threat of death can strike at any time through unknown perils or age. While in one the figure of old age is grieving, in the other painting, the embracing couple are perched warily on a decorative, yet symbolic precipice.

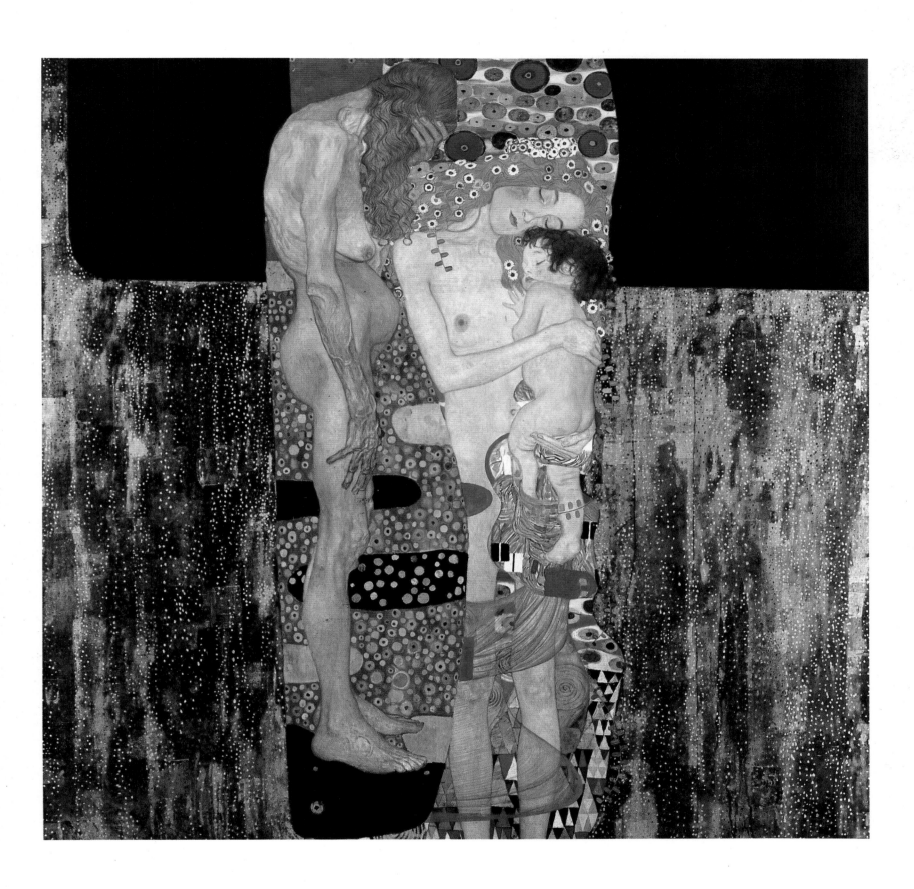

Portrait of Margaret Stonborough-Wittgenstein,

1905

Oil on canvas
70⅞×35 inches (180×90cm)
Bayerische Staatsgemäldesammlungen,
Neue Pinakothek, Munich

It is easy to fall into the trap of believing that Klimt met with no resistance to or criticism of his portraits. In fact in 1908 Emilie Flöge, who for reasons unrecorded was unhappy with Klimt's portrait of her, sold the picture to the Historisches Museum der Stadt Wien. The next to refuse her portrait was Margaret Wittgenstein.

Karl Wittgenstein, who commissioned his daughter's portrait, was one of the great steel barons and a patron of the arts. As well as supporting the composers Brahms and Mahler, Wittgenstein helped finance the construction of the Secession Building. In 1904 Wittgenstein offered Klimt 5000 guilders (the payment of which Klimt deferred until completion) to paint his daughter's portrait. Having made a series of preliminary drawings, Klimt had nearly completed the portrait when he showed it to the family. Agreeing to make certain amendments, Klimt then asked to show both the portrait and the drawings in an exhibition.

By this time, however, Margaret had married an American (hence Stonborough-Wittgenstein), had moved to Berlin and was expecting her first child. Since she was now no longer able to sit for him, Klimt made alterations to the background only. The finished painting hung for only a short time at the Wittgensteins' home before it was placed on permanent loan in Austria, eventually being acquired by the Neue Pinakothek in Munich.

The organic ornamentation that appears in *Portrait of Emilie Flöge* is here transformed into pseudo-architectural forms and once again the hands and face of the model stand out from the rest of the painting in their treatment. Margaret's expression and bearing makes her appear somewhat aloof, but with an air of expectancy (similar to that in the *Portrait of Sonja Knips*) and somewhat removed from reality, not at all like the real Margaret who was known as a sharp-minded woman with an interest in science and mathematics.

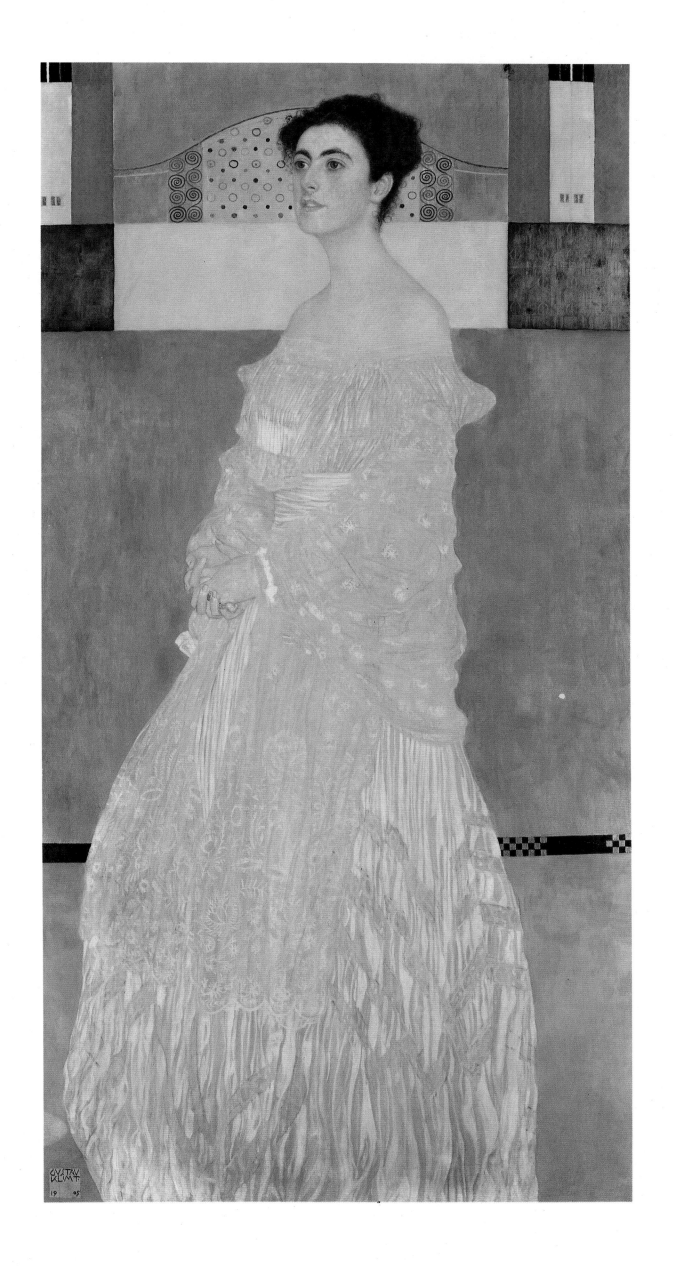

Portrait of Fritza Riedler, 1906

Oil on canvas
60¼×52⅜ inches (153×133cm)
Österreichische Galerie, Vienna

The Wittgenstein portrait of 1905 (page 65) has been seen as a transitional work in which it is possible to see Klimt's development from the Impressionism of *The Portrait of Sonja Knips* to the more decorative manner of his work after the *Stoclet Frieze*.

This decorative tendency is far more pronounced in the *Portrait of Fritza Riedler*, especially in the repeated 'eye' motif in the pattern of the armchair and the curious semi-circular mosaic panel behind Fritza's head. These two-dimensional decorative forms contain the figure and make it appear immobile and further flatten the already shallow picture space. This painting also coincides with the beginning of Klimt's so-called 'golden period': in the background there is a self-contained area of gold. Furthermore, this picture is the first of the square, or near-square portraits of the 'golden period'.

The mosaic panel by Fritza's head, variously interpreted as a headdress, crown and halo, is a motif that Klimt evidently derived from studying Velázquez's portraits (page 12) of the Spanish royal family on display in the Kunsthistorisches Museum in Vienna. As a 'headdress' the panel serves as a device to reflect the prestige of the sitter as society woman as well as being a balancing compositional element.

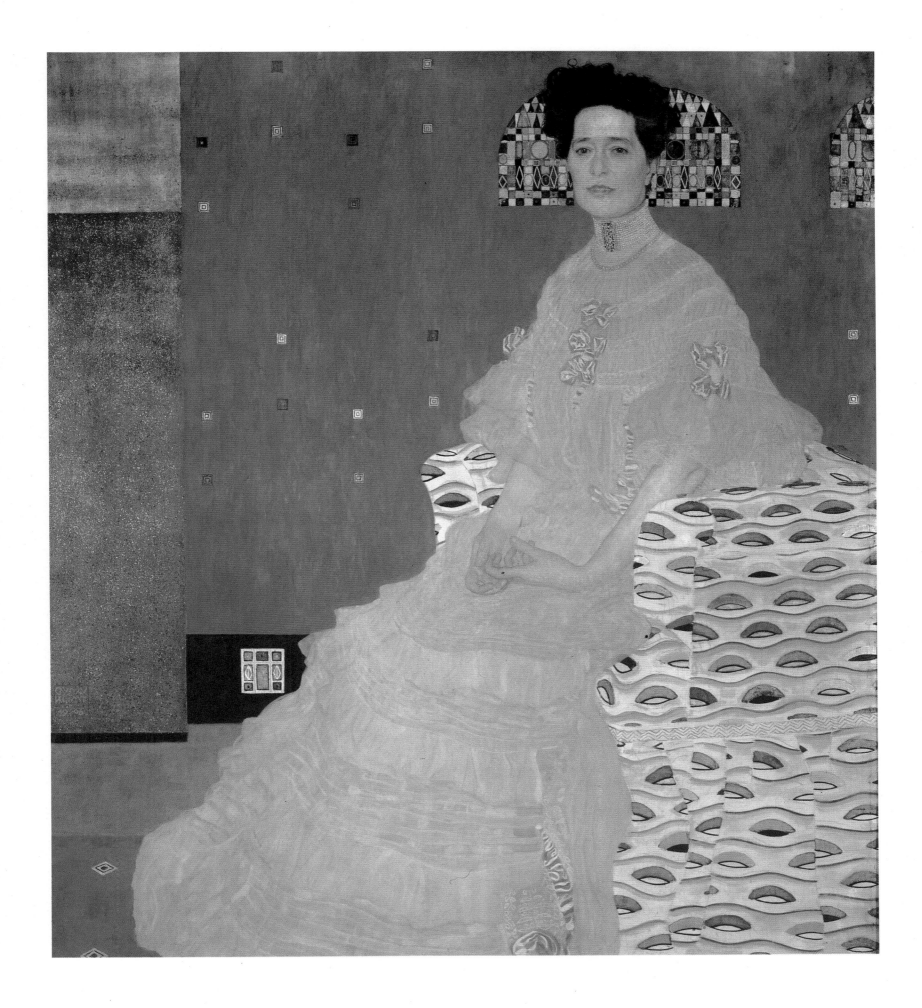

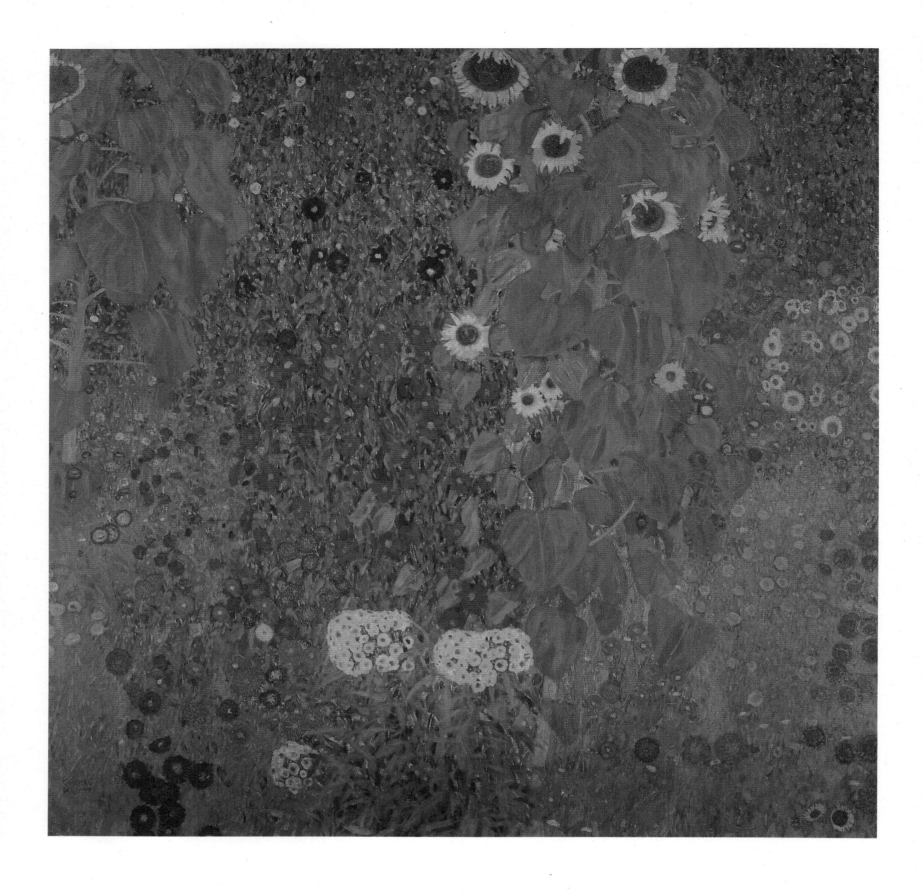

Cottage Garden with Sunflowers, c. 1905-06

Oil on canvas
43⅓ × 43⅓ inches (110×110cm)
Österreichische Galerie, Vienna

The biggest event since the Klimt group withdrew from the Vienna Secession in 1905 was the first Kunstschau in 1908, where, as well as *The Kiss*, Klimt exhibited *Cottage Garden with Sunflowers*.

Despite the absence of gold, this painting is no less jewel-like with its arrangement of strong, clear colors. An abundance of flowers and leaves of varying sizes, shapes and colors vie in the two-dimensional space, producing the visual effect of 'infinity' that Klimt showed in his paintings of lakes and forests.

Popular with the Symbolists, the sunflower as a motif embodied a wide range of meanings from worship and adoration to fickleness and unreliability, since the flower is both a slave to the sun yet constantly changes its position. In Klimt's painting however, such analogies are absent, yet the flowers are so abundant that they seem to be a tribute to nature.

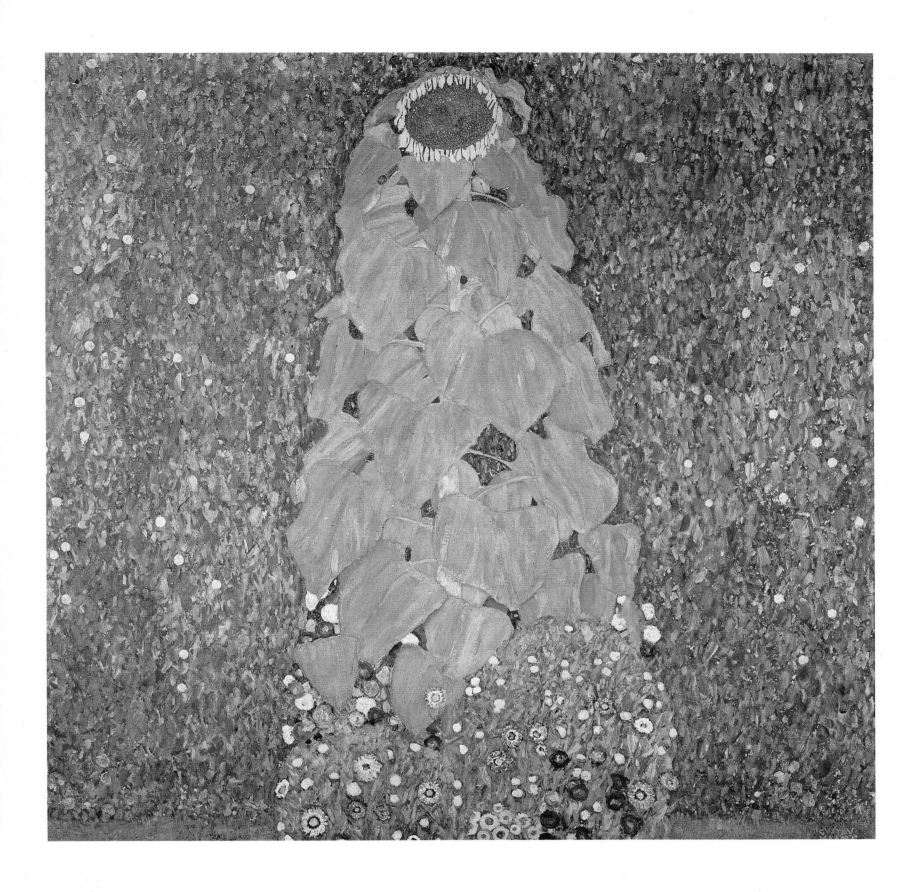

The Sunflower, 1906-07

Oil on canvas
43⅓×43⅓ inches (110×110cm)
Österreichische Galerie, Vienna

Exhibited at the first Kunstschau in 1908, along with *Cottage Garden with Sunflowers* (page 68), *The Sunflower* echoes the triangual shape of the earlier landscape *Flower Garden* (1905-06) as well as the poses of many of his subjects in his portraits and allegorical compositions, for instance, *Fritza Riedler* (1906; page 67) and *Hope II* (1907-08; page 74). Most of all, *The Sunflower* is the botanical counterpart to *The Kiss* (1907).

The sunflower at the center of the picture towers alone and appears to be drooping its head against a background of greenery. Once again the depth of the pic-

ture space has been restricted to a shallow area. Unlike those other famous sunflowers by Vincent van Gogh which are still-life representations, Klimt's *The Sunflower* is a landscape.

The critic chronicler of the Secession in Vienna, Ludwig Hevesi (who, incidentally, supplied the motto carved in Olbrich's building: *Der Zeit ihre Kunst, der Kunst ihre Freiheit*), has probably not been surpassed in his comparison of *The Sunflower* to a 'fairy in love.' Never before had nature, its quietness and its pulsating life, been expressed in so direct and powerful a way.

69

Portrait of Adèle Bloch-Bauer, 1907

Oil on canvas
$54\frac{1}{3} \times 54\frac{1}{3}$ inches (138×138cm)
Österreichische Galerie, Vienna

This portrait represents Klimt's 'golden period' more fully than any other painting, and is also the last portrait in the golden style. Preliminary drawings of Adèle Bloch-Bauer, the wife of industrialist Ferdinand Bloch, come from the years between 1903 and 1904, but the portrait was not completed for some four years.

Here the characteristics of Klimt's style are carried to their extreme: naturalistically rendered hands and features are set against a two-dimensional background which becomes merged with the armchair's Mycenean-inspired scroll decoration, the mosaics and Adèle's dress.

The eye motif seen in Fritza Riedler's chair here reappears in a central panel in Adèle's gown. Apart from the face and arms which appear almost detached from her body and the small area of green floor separated from the background wall by a chequerboard skirting, the picture consists almost entirely of gold and golden decoration.

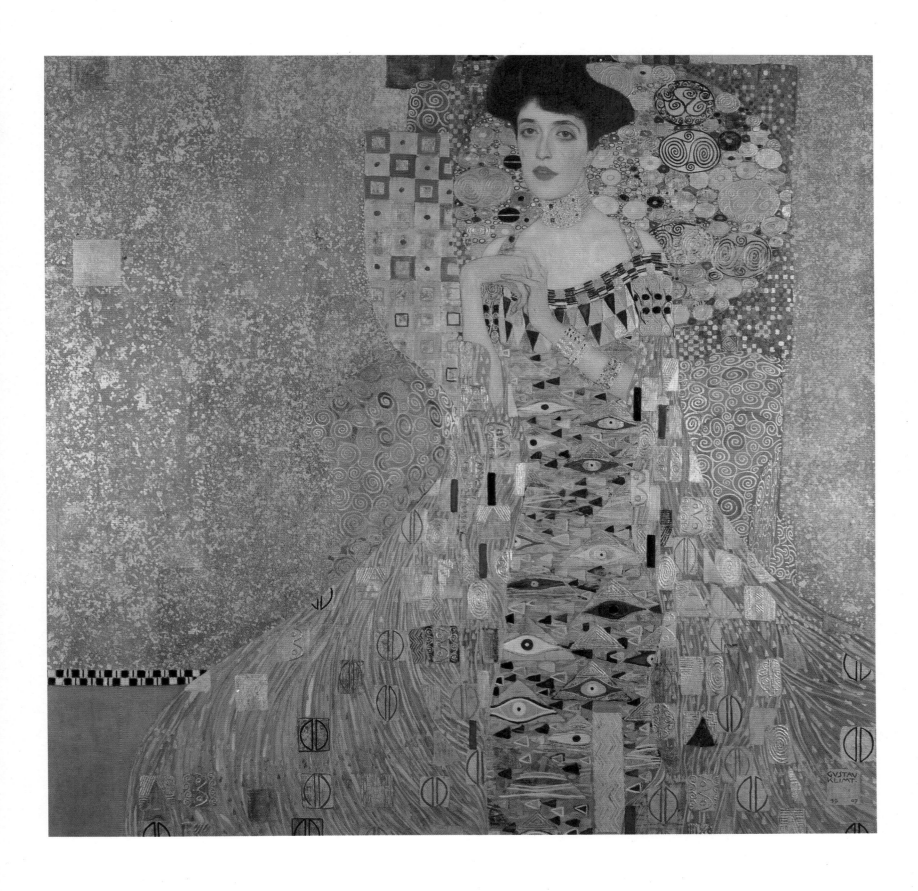

Danae, c. 1907-08
Oil on canvas
$30\frac{1}{3}\times32\frac{5}{8}$ inches (77×83cm)
Private collection

The legend of Danae has often been depicted by artists: Acrisius, Danae's father, had been told by an oracle that his grandson would kill him. To forestall this event, Acrisius imprisoned his daughter in a dungeon guarded by gods. Despite these precautions, Danae bore a son, Perseus, by Zeus who 'visited' Danaë disguised as a shower of gold. Perseus would eventually fulfill the oracle's prophecy.

In his interpretation, Klimt has concentrated on the actual moment of the conception of Perseus: between the raised legs of the slumbering Danae appears the shower of gold. Within this work, Klimt combined explorations into both Jugendstil painting and the theme of female sexuality.

As in many other paintings, Klimt has portrayed the woman overcome by sleep and thus unaware of anything outside herself. The viewer becomes a 'voyeur' of Danae, who is erotic even in her sleep.

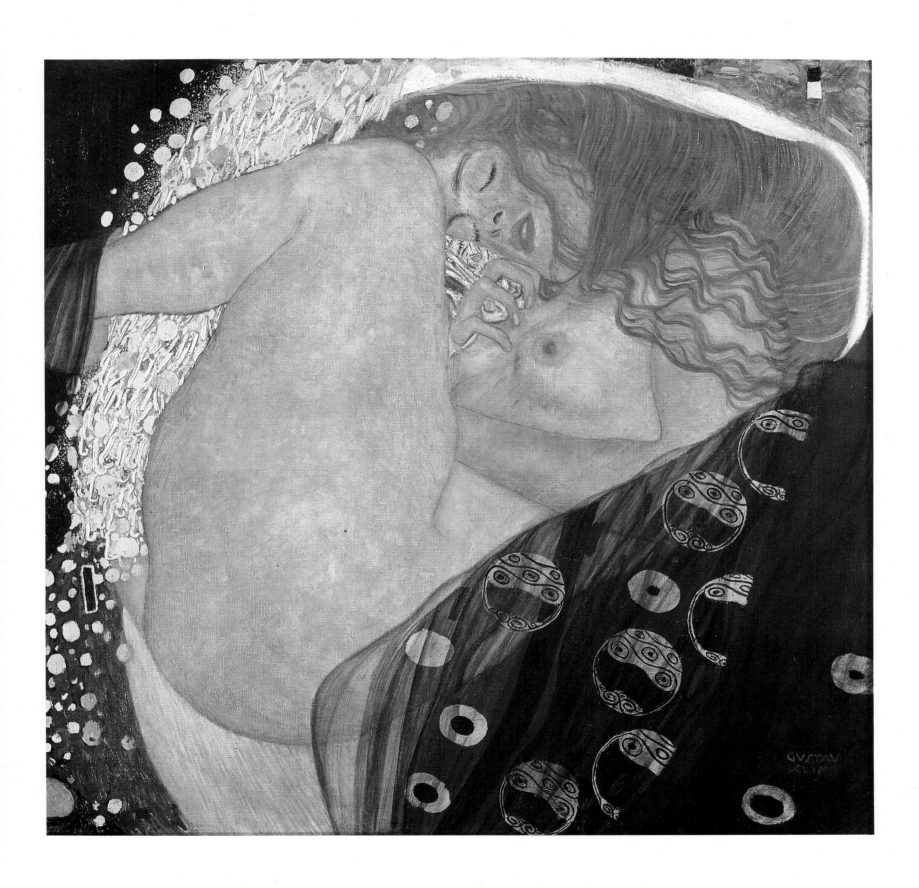

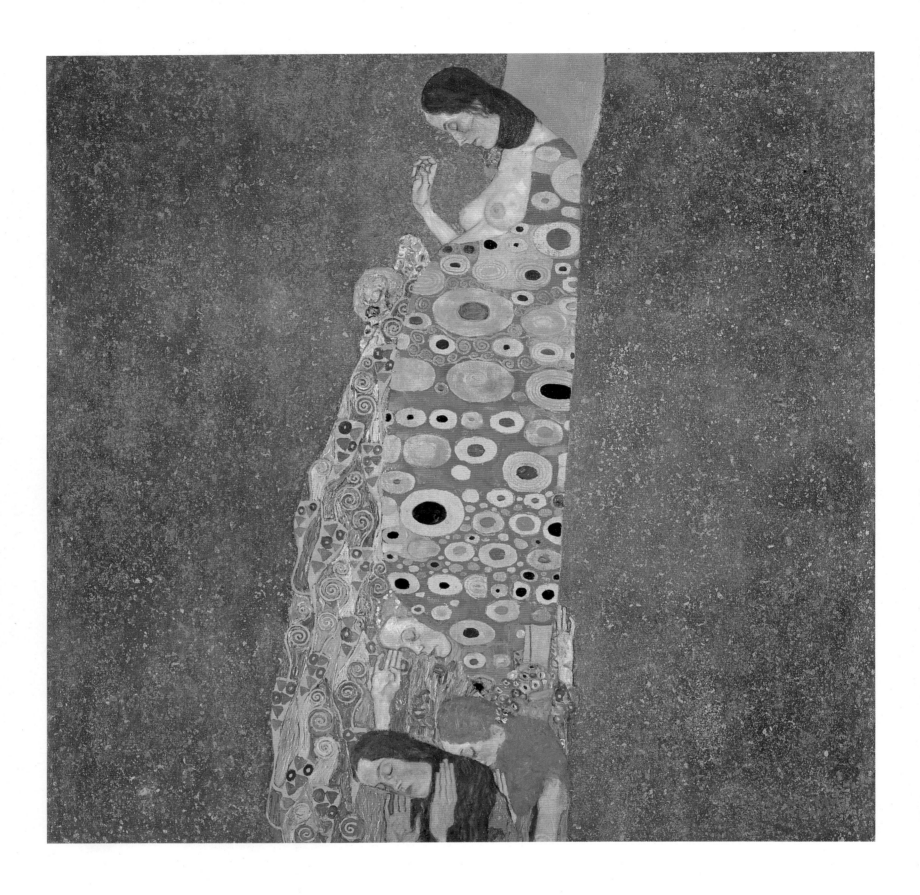

Hope II, 1907-08

Oil on canvas
43⅓×43⅓ inches (110×110cm)
Collection, the Museum of Modern Art,
New York

When Klimt took up the theme of the pregnant woman again in *Hope II* he considerably altered both the style and the symbolic forms of the earlier version. The tall rectangular format of *Hope I* (page 50) is replaced by the square canvas; the three grim faces that lurk in the darkness of the background have given way to three sleeping women and the skull now appears to have been placed directly on the woman's pregnant body.

Gone also is the eye contact between the woman in *Hope I* and the viewer. In the second version, the woman, like the sleeping Danae, is completely absorbed in

herself, unaware of any other presence. Above all, she is no longer nude. Almost all her body has become a flat decorative pattern. What little background there was in *Hope I* has disappeared completely. The strong two-dimensional organization of space also appears in Klimt's garden pictures in the same period.

Where *Hope I* is a symbolic representation of fertility while at the same time highlighting the fears or 'angst' represented by the sinister faces, *Hope II* is less ambiguous for it merely re-states the central theme of the eternal cycle of life and death as a natural process.

Judith II (Salome), 1909

$70 \times 18\frac{1}{8}$ inches (178×46cm)
Galleria d'Arte Moderna Venice

As in *Danae* where Klimt avoided re-
telling the legend in order to represent
Danae herself, *Judith II* is a representation of the woman. Like the earlier version, *Judith II* is also frequently referred
to as *Salome*, the archetypal femme fatale,
and like many of Klimt's female figures
painted at this time, she faces to the right.
The undulating curves of her body and
dress make her appear as though she is
dancing, justifying her subtitle of Salome.
With her finger tips she holds the sack out
of which pokes the severed head of Holo-
fernes/John the Baptist.

Compared to *Judith I*, this Judith is less
threatening and less seductive. Nor does
she engage the spectator with her look nor
hold the severed head like a trophy. The
ambiguity is heightened by the subtitle: it
is difficult to see whether the figure in
Judith II is the Judith who has used her
sexuality to lure Holofernes to his death,
or the Salome who orders the head of the
Baptist because he refuses to succumb to
her sexuality.

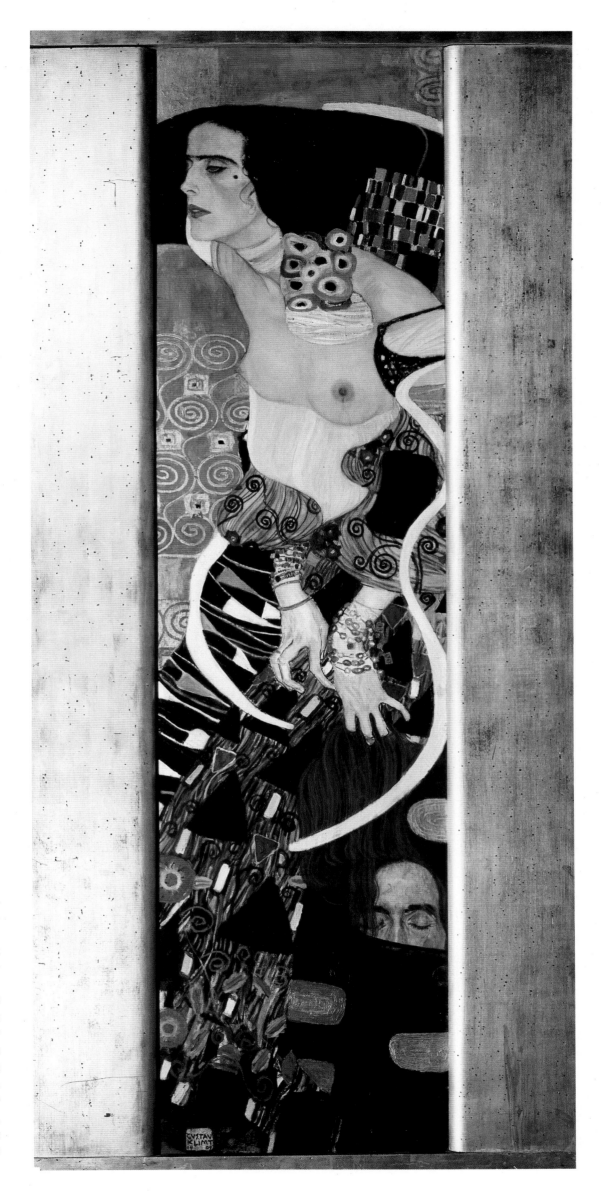

75

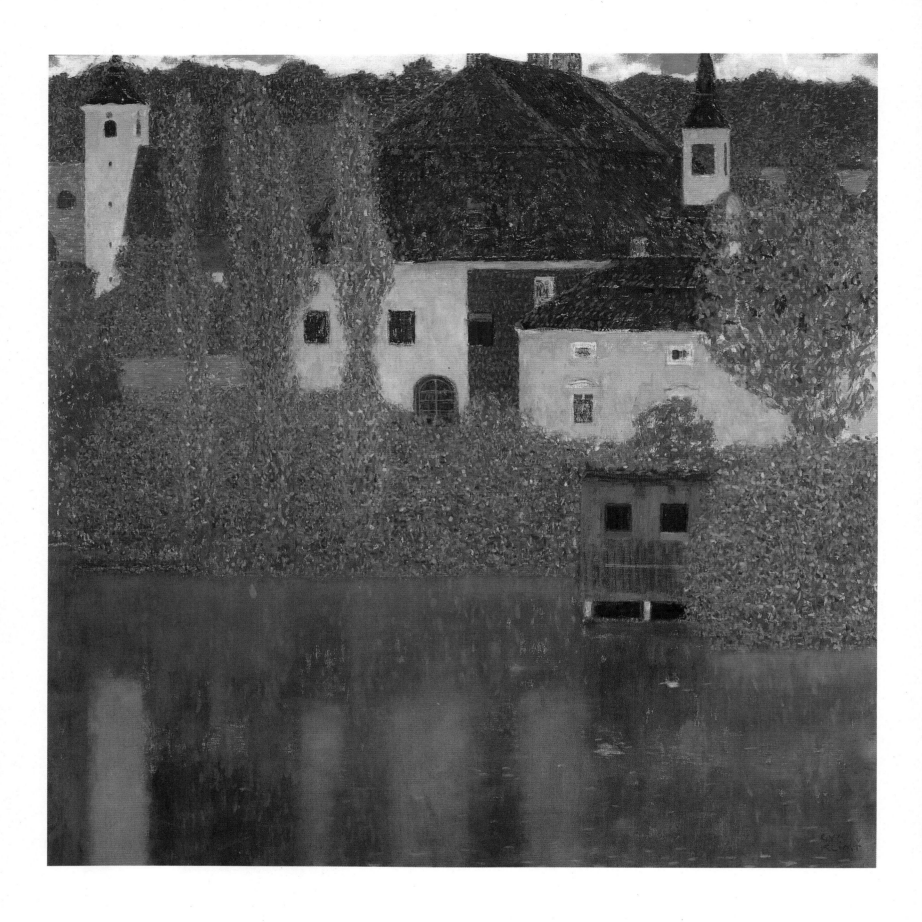

Schloss Kammer on the Attersee I, c. 1908

Oil on canvas
43⅓×43⅓ inches (110×110cm)
National Gallery, Prague

Around 1908 Klimt reached a turning point in his conception of landscape painting. From this point, the solution to the problem of incorporating an architectural motif into the landscape became more varied. In 1908 the *Schloss Kammer on the Attersee I* (also known as *Schloss on the Water*) was exhibited at the National Gallery in Prague, where it remains today.

The castle obviously had an attraction for Klimt, for he painted three further versions, two of which are again from the water. While the composer Gustav Mahler had a passion for motor cars, Klimt enjoyed a motor boat, and like Monet had

done, he would often paint from his boat on the lake where, no doubt, he would be free from any interruption.

The architectural elements in *Schloss Kammer I* are presented like a façade in strict frontality. On closer inspection however, we do see the foreshortened main roof and the turrets of the Schloss. The Schloss, the small boathouse with its four dark openings, and the layers of vegetation are all reflected in the lake below. In the subsequent version that Klimt painted, *Schloss Kammer on the Attersee II* (1909-10), although the castle is depicted without the water, the strict frontality remains.

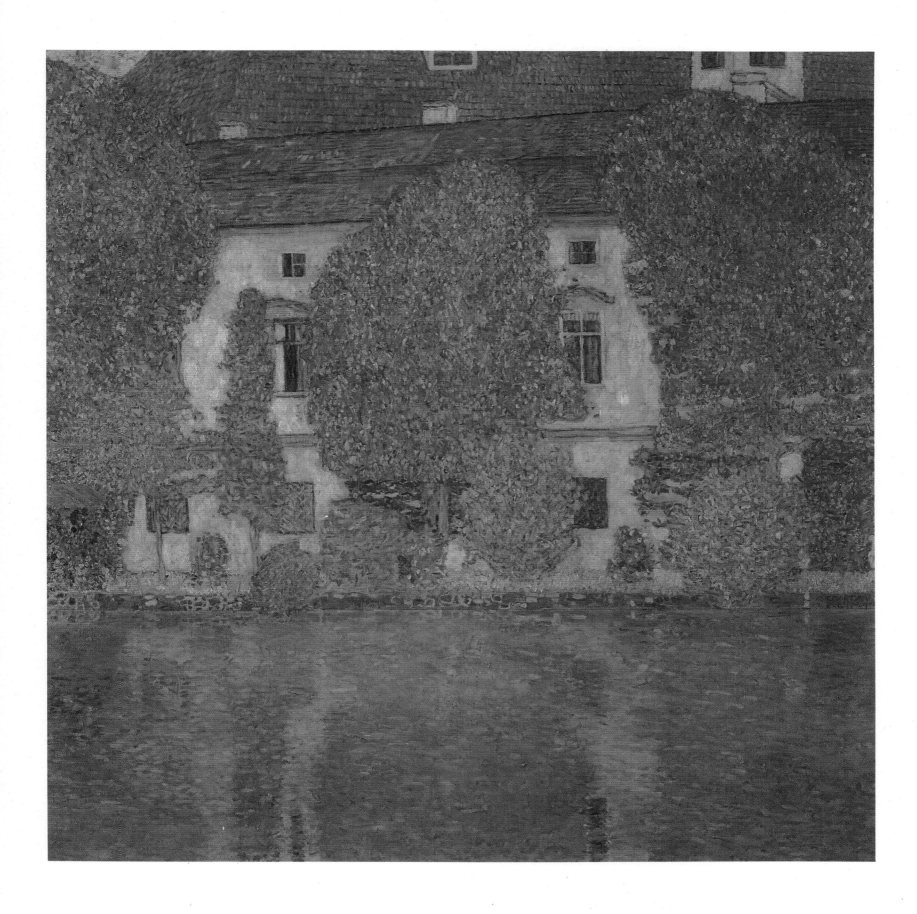

Schloss Kammer on the Attersee III, 1910

Oil on canvas
43⅓×43⅓ inches (110×110cm)
Österreichische Galerie, Vienna

By habit a studio painter, Klimt nevertheless shows his mastery at plein-air painting. He is known to have left unfinished pictures concealed in the undergrowth in order to avoid carrying the canvasses to and fro. A man governed by routine who was also extremely sensitive to any disurbance would only paint out of doors when he was able to have the seclusion to allow him to work uninterrupted. No doubt by painting in his boat on the lake, he was given this seclusion.

In this, the third version of the Schloss Kammer, we again see the interplay between frontal elements and those in perspective: we see both sides of the chimneys while at the same time assuming a central viewpoint when looking at the façade. At the top left, the red tiled roof of the Schloss has been flattened and depicted frontally. This 'simultaneous' display of the sides of the architectural subjects is derived from the canons of Egyptian art in which all the important aspects of human body (or indeed the bodies' material possessions) were depicted frontally. As Egyptian art was inextricably linked with the cult of the dead, tomb paintings were the means of providing the deceased with all things necessary for his afterlife. In order to enjoy his new existence to the full, human bodies were depicted with the head in profile but with a full-face eye, while a pond with a garden surrounding it would be shown in both plan and elevation simultaneously (we see the pond from a bird's eye view, while the trees are seen in elevation, arranged around the pond as though a wind has blown them over). This way individual elements and their interrelation would be recognizable.

77

The Kiss, 1907-09

Oil on canvas
70⅞×70⅞ inches (180×180cm)
Österreichische Galerie, Vienna

In Room 22 of the Kunstschau in May 1908, Klimt's large painting *The Kiss* was exhibited for the first time. In this work we see the culmination of his mosaic manner using mixed media in the ultimate decorative splendor. The stylization of clothes noticeable in the earlier portraits here reaches its zenith in pure surface pattern. Furthermore, *The Kiss* is the most elaborate working of the theme of the embrace first seen in *Love*, the *Beethoven Frieze* and the *Stoclet Frieze*.

For once, Klimt's contribution to modern European art was recognized at the time: before the Kunstschau closed *The Kiss* was purchased for the Austrian nation.

Perched on a flowery precipice, the two lovers are shown surrounded by an aura of gold, similar to the one surrounding the figures in the final scene of the *Beethoven Frieze*. The flat background gives a sense of an indeterminate location and removes the figures from any reference point in space or time.

The ornamental symbolism of the garments has led the painting to be interpreted as a symbol of the union between the sexes: the man has been given harsh rectangular forms (a black rectangle also appears between the legs of Danaë) while the woman has been given ovoid ornamentation. Yet the couple, despite their embrace, remain unrelated and distanced from each other. The extreme angle of the woman's head – anatomically impossible – makes her appear utterly passive if not dead; yet her hand is still clasped and her toes cling to the edge of the flowery cliff. Here it is the man who dominates and initiates the action of the kiss.

Whatever interpretations are given (a symbol of union or the depiction of what can never be fulfilled because of the tensions between man and woman) the fascination for *The Kiss* is comparable to that which surrounds the *Mona Lisa*. Perhaps because the complexities of meaning in *The Kiss* have never been fully resolved, it remains Klimt's most popular painting.

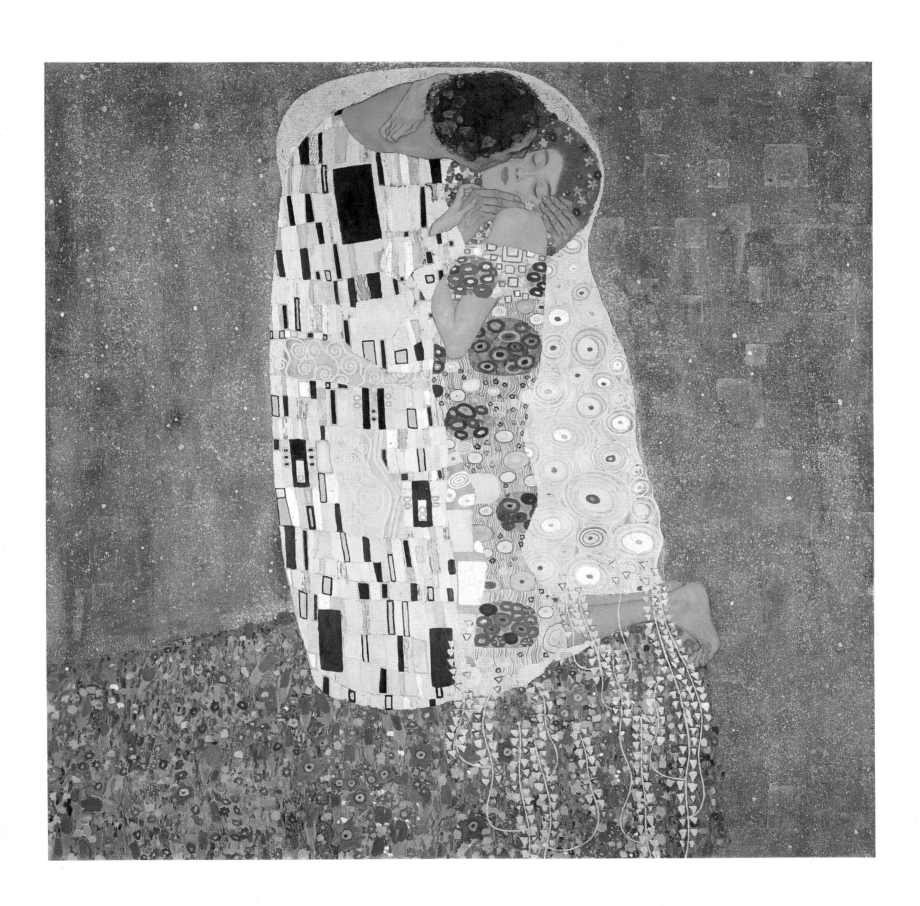

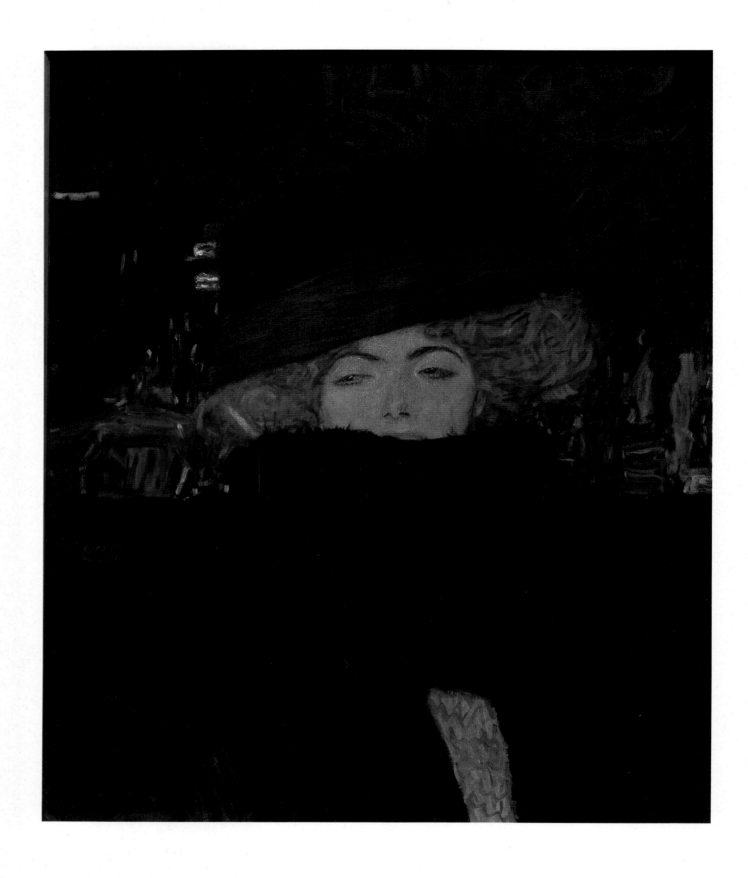

Lady with a Feather Hat, 1910
Oil on canvas
$31 \times 24\frac{7}{8}$ inches (79×63cm)
Private collection, USA

Between 1909 and 1910 a radical change in Klimt's style becomes apparent: except in the as-yet unfinished *Stoclet Frieze*, he stopped using gold and his brushstrokes became bolder and wider. In two uncommissioned portraits of unknown models from 1910, *Lady with a Feather Hat* and *Lady with a Hat and Feather Boa* (page 80), Klimt relinquished all the ornamentation so characteristic of his early style. Although it was to return in his later works, it was in quite a different form.

In contrast to Klimt's portraits of wealthy Viennese society belles, the woman in *Lady with a Feather Hat*, in spite of her elaborate hat and fur stole, is more akin in spirit to the figure in Degas' *The Glass of Absinthe* (1876) and rather than the sense we get of 'looking up' at the society portraits, Klimt has structured this portrait in such a manner that the spectator assumes a higher position, thus looking down on the woman.

Like many women in Klimt's allegorical compositions, this woman is unaware of the spectator's presence.

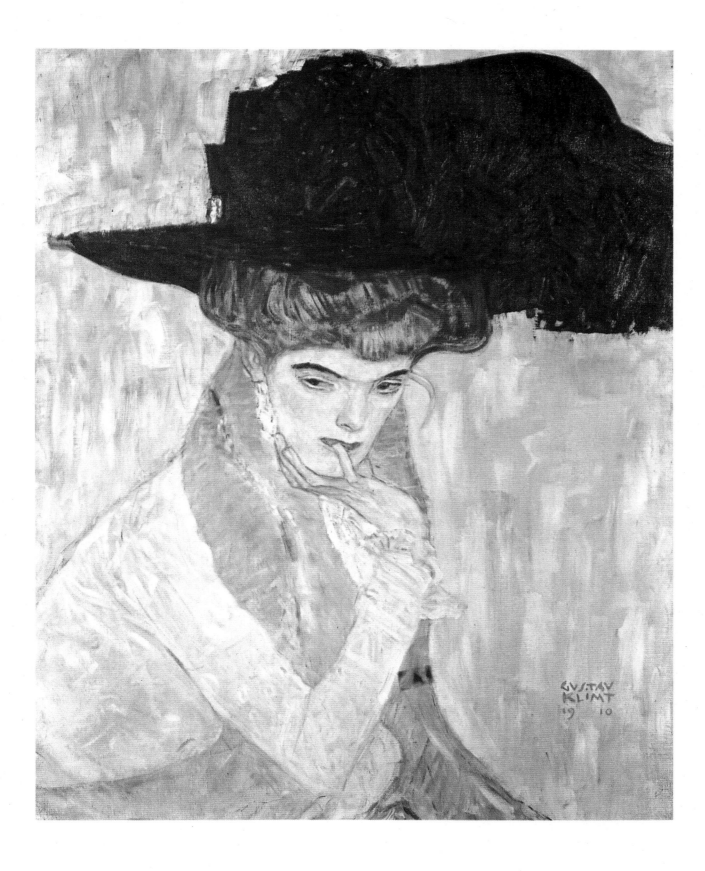

Lady with a Hat and Feather Boa, 1910

Oil on canvas
27⅛×21 inches (69×55cm)
Österreichische Galerie, Vienna

This portrait, once again uncommissioned and of an unknown model, is very different from those which precede it. In the first instance, it is one of the few portraits, like the *Portrait of Sonja Knips*, that has some sense of a location in the background. Although the background is covered by the head and shoulders of the lady, there is in the green tones the outlines of a town.

Her face is framed by the hat but also half covered by the feather boa and once again there is no eye contact made with the specator. Like the woman in *Lady with a Feather Hat* (page 80), this woman appears more real than the woman in Klimt's commissioned portraits; both are more tangible and less static.

It seems as though Klimt had two different approaches in his depictions of women – a fantasy of decorative opulence for wealthy women and a more direct realism for the women who inhabited the demi-monde of Vienna.

The Park, before 1910
Oil on canvas
43⅓×43⅓ inches (110×110cm)
Collection, the Museum of Modern Art,
New York
Gertrude A Mellon Fund

In this picture, painted shortly before 1910, Klimt once again takes the image of trees as his motif. Compared with *Beech Wood I*, where the tree trunks occupy most of the picture surface, here it is the leafy tops of the trees that cover the surface of the painting. Yet like the tree trunks of the earlier picture, the tree tops once again extend infinitely in all directions.

Although Klimt did not use the same rigid pointillism as Seurat, where spots of color blend optically rather than physically, Klimt's technique in this painting is nevertheless derived from the Neo-Impressionists.

The most striking feature of this painting is the uniformity of the surface structure and the way depth – a great distance, in fact – is suggested without using illusionistic means, but simply by using the overlapping effect in the crown of the trees and their trunks.

Portrait of Adèle Bloch-Bauer II, 1912

Oil on canvas
$74\frac{4}{5} \times 47\frac{1}{4}$ inches (190×120cm)
Österreichische Galerie, Vienna

The sixth exhibition of the Secession in January 1900, although it did not meet with much enthusiasm from the Viennese public, was immensely important to Klimt. The exhibition was devoted entirely to Japanese art and awakened in Klimt an interest in Oriental art which he began to collect. The motifs which he took from oriental paintings, vases and textiles appear in the backgrounds of the later society portraits.

In this, the second portrait of Adèle Bloch-Bauer, Klimt returns to a much lighter palette than used in *Lady with a Hat and Feather Boa* (page 81), and also echoes the geometrical ornamentation of the 'golden period' works with parts being filled with Chinese-inspired images and motifs. This portrait is also the first of the strongly decorative frontal portraits of Klimt's later period.

Here, the rigid frontal pose of Adèle Bloch-Bauer makes her appear like a doll while her large hat is like the halo motif that we have seen in the earlier portraits.

In these, the later years of Klimt's life, the emphasis on pattern, decoration and color is still very much in evidence, but there is an increasing concern for more geometrical compositions and forms.

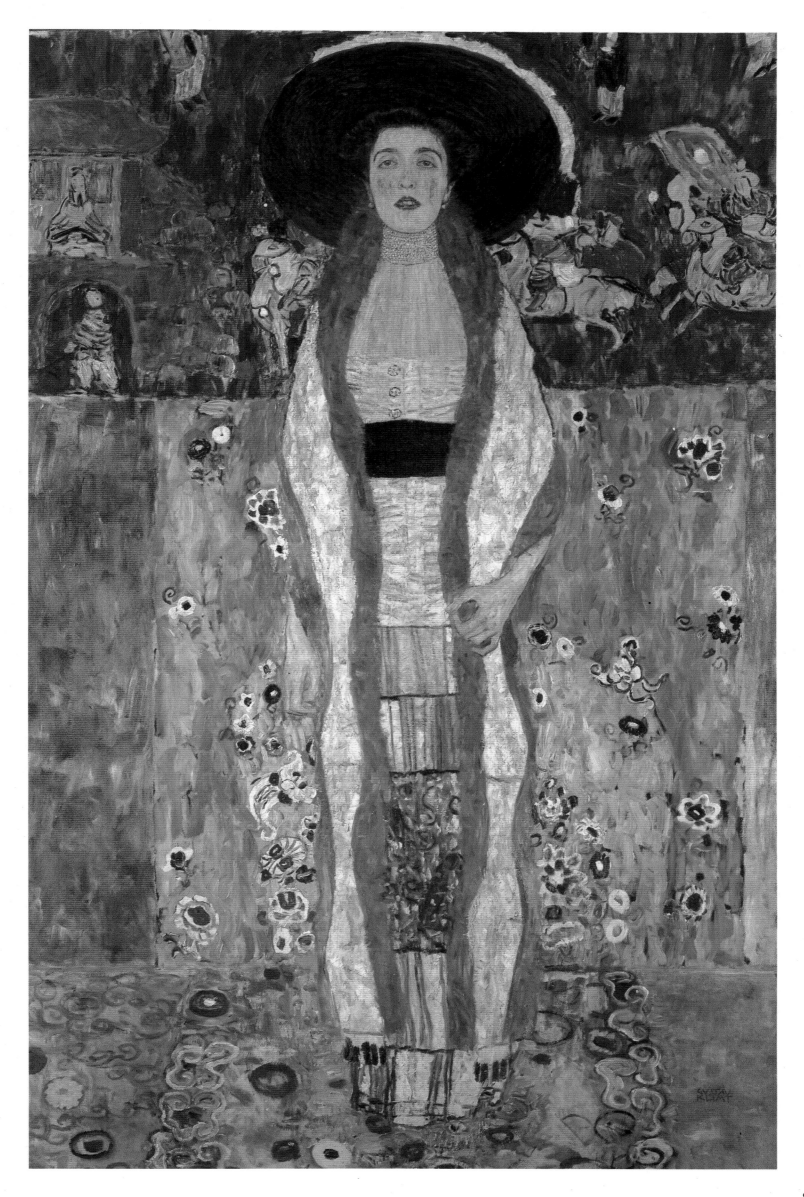

Avenue in the Park of the Schloss Kammer, 1912

Oil on canvas
43⅓×43⅓ inches (110×110cm)
Österreichische Galerie, Vienna

The square format of this painting has been skillfully offset by the shortened perspective and the assymetrical arrangement of the trees lining the avenue to the castle, while at the same time Klimt retains the strict frontality. The heavier impasto and the twisted forms of the trees remind us of the influence of the Post-Impressionists, particularly in the heavy outlines of the Nabis and Van Gogh.

Klimt had been familiar with the work of the Post-Impressionists since 1903, when the sixteenth exhibition of the Secession included works by Cézanne, Gauguin and Van Gogh. In the same year the Secession acquired Van Gogh's *Plain of Auvers-sur-Oise*, painted in 1890, and presented the painting to the Modern gallery. A second large exhibition of Van Gogh's work took place at the Galerie Mienthke in 1907.

Klimt, however, was not an artist to pick up on a style of influence and use it immediately in his own work. Over the years he would slowly assimilate and absorb these influences until they emerged in his own paintings, though still identifiable, as individual forms. This gradual process can also be seen in the way the effects of seeing the mosaics at San Vitale in Ravenna in 1903 emerge only later in the *Stoclet Frieze.*

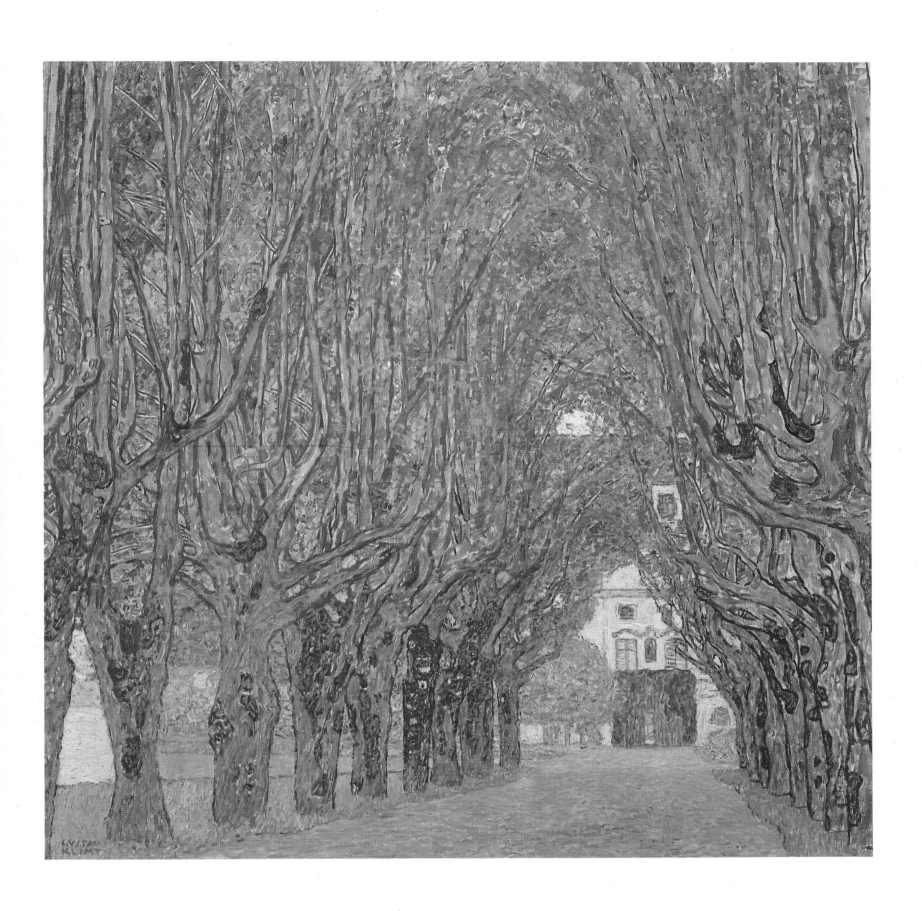

Portrait of Mäda Primavesi,

c. 1912

Oil on canvas
59×43½ inches (150×110.5cm)
The Metropolitan Museum of Art, New
York, Gift of Andre and Clara Mertens,
in memory of her mother, Jenny
Pulitzer Steiner, 1964

Once a year (sometimes twice a year)
Klimt paid a visit to the home of the Primavesi family in Olmitz. Otto Primavesi,
a banker, stepped in as the financial
backer of the Wiener Werkstätte when
Fritz Wärndofer emigrated to America.
Originally patrons of Josef Hoffmann,
the Primavesi family entertained their
house guests each year with a *Schwin-
delfest*. Klimt may have been introduced
to the family by Hoffmann, his long-
standing colleague, or through Emile
Flöge, whose fashion salon, the *Casa Piccolo*, included among its clients Mäda Primavesi and her mother Eugenia.

In addition to purchasing several of
Klimt's works, Otto Primavesi commissioned this portrait of his daughter. Once
again using a strictly frontal format,
Klimt has caught Mäda as the girl on the
threshold of womanhood. At the same
time that she is assured, her feet planted
firmly on the carpet, her arms twisted and
hidden behind her back make her appear
somewhat gauche.

A geometric arrangement of the background divides the picture into two sections of what appears at first sight to be a
pink wall and an oriental carpet, but,
because there is no diminution of the sizes
of the pattern, the background remains
flat. Mäda could just as easily be standing
at the very edge of a rug with a wavy-line
border against a flat backdrop of a decorative screen.

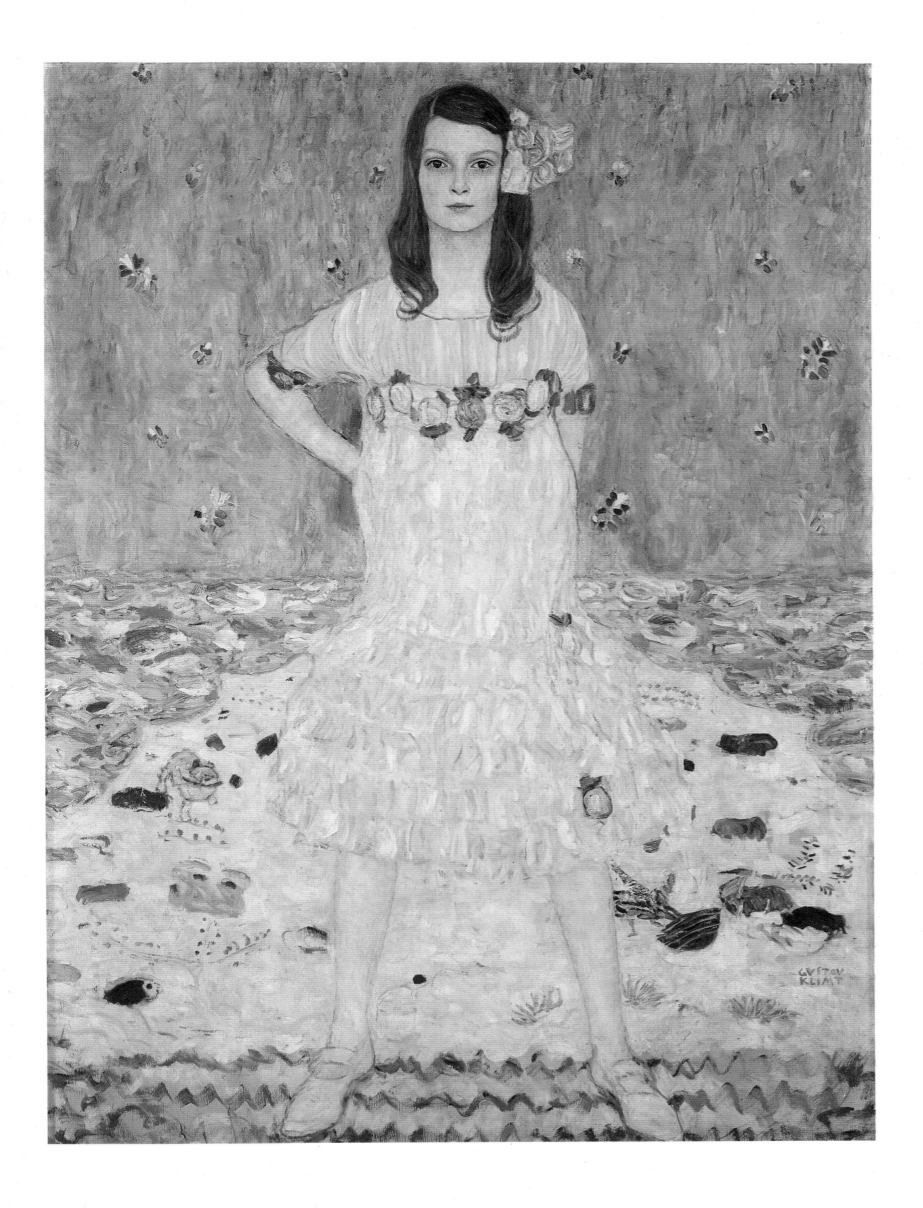

Death and Life, before 1911,
reworked 1916

Oil on canvas
70×78 inches (178×198cm)
Collection Dr Rudolf Leopold, Vienna

In this painting, Klimt offers a further interpretation of the theme of the cycle of life and death. The group of sleeping figures on the right of the picture are related both to the sleeping woman and child in *The Three Ages of Woman* and to the figures in the chains of struggling humanity in the University commissions. Thematically, this painting is also related to the two paintings of Hope.

Old age, decay and death, earlier representated by the old woman (*Three Ages of Woman*; page 63) and the sinister faces and Skull in *Hope I* (page 50) and *Hope II* (page 74) are now replaced by the club-bearing figure of death himself, while the sleeping figures remain blissfully unaware of his approach. Furthermore, Klimt has structured the composition in such a manner that death and the sleeping figures occupy their own individual spaces, like bubbles of existence.

It is also possible to see this painting as yet one more working of the 'embrace' theme: the muscular form of the male figure echoes that in the final scene of the *Beethoven Frieze*. Yet here the love is neither ecstatic nor triumphant, but an insufficient comforter against the onset of age and decay.

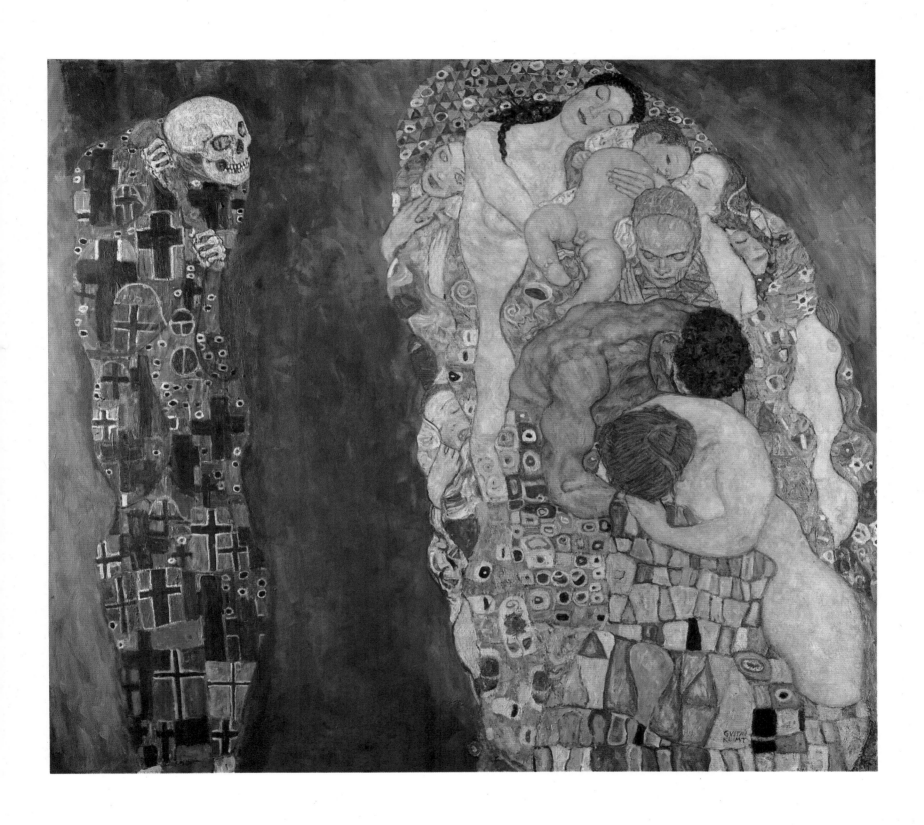

The Virgin, 1913

Oil on canvas
$74\frac{7}{8} \times 78\frac{3}{4}$ inches (190×200 cm)
National Gallery, Prague

Once again Klimt returned to the motif of the intertwined group of slumbering figures that are familiar from his earlier works. Even without their titles, it would be possible for the viewer to uncover the allegorical meanings of the earlier works, but in Klimt's later paintings, reading or finding meaning becomes more difficult since there is less action and less allegory.

The only, very tenuous, clue to the content lies in the symbolism of the color of the central sleeping figure's dress. By tradition in religious paintings, blue (usually ultramarine, or azurite, a less expensive pigment) was the color reserved in art for the gown of the Virgin Mary. A motif that we have seen before in the *Stoclet Frieze*, the Mycenean scroll motif, here reappears in the pattern in the virgin's dress, while a similar treatment of flowers also can be seen in the landscapes and garden paintings of the same period.

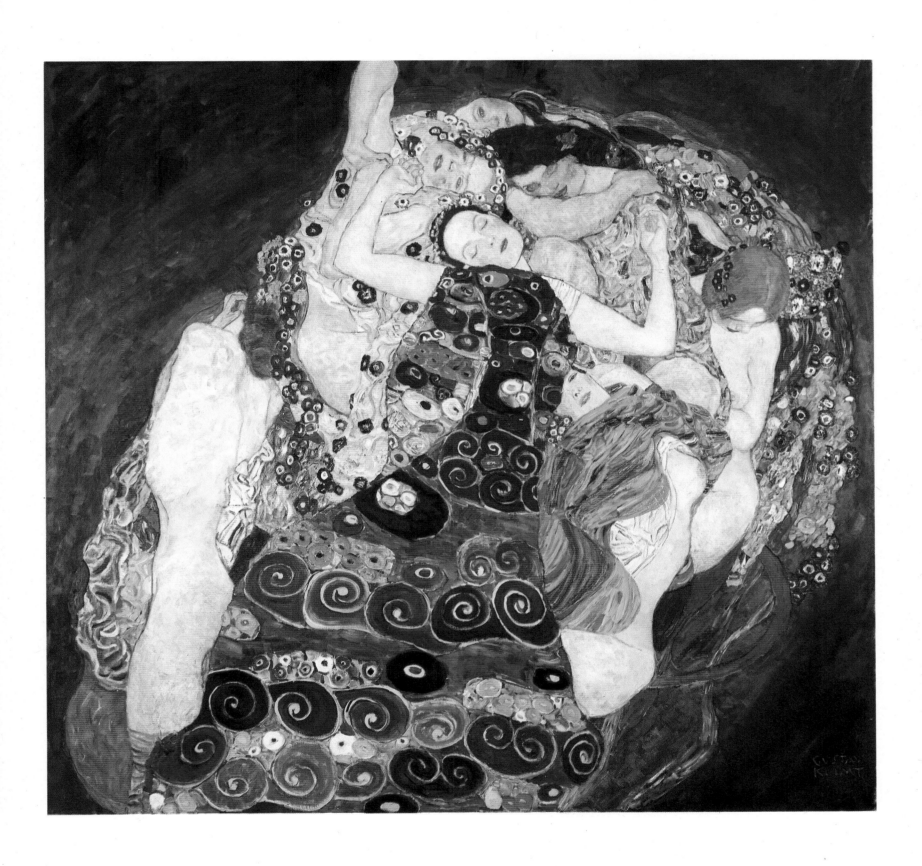

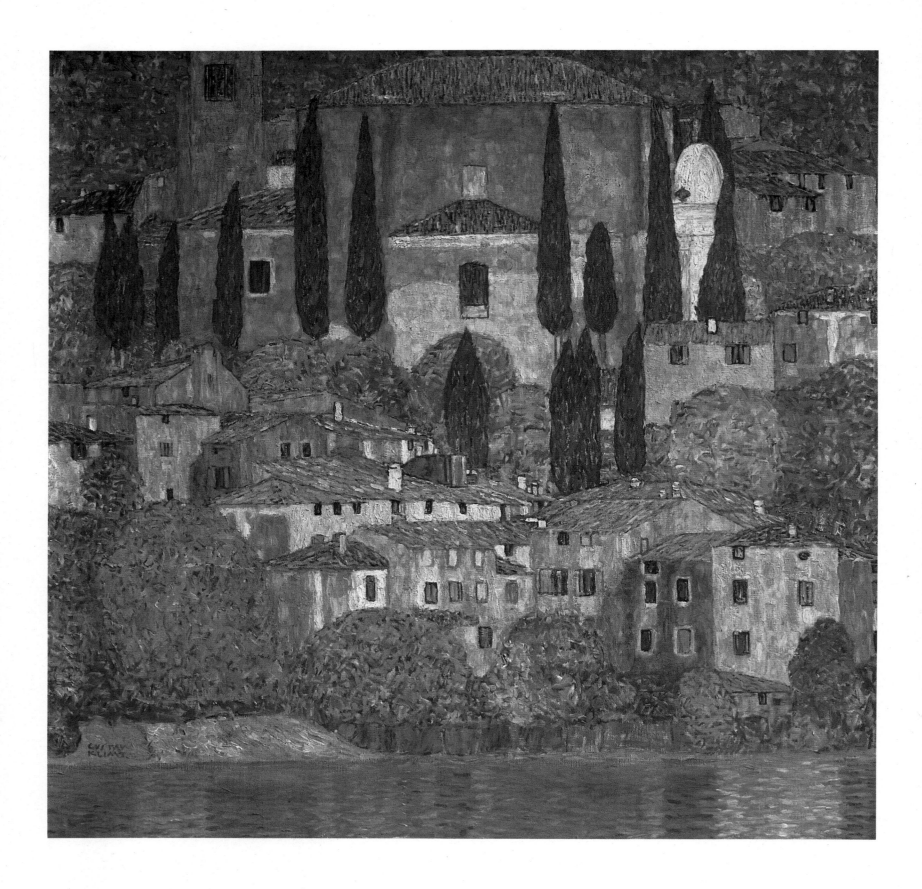

Church at Cassone, 1913

Oil on canvas
43⅓ × 43⅓ inches (110 × 110cm)
Private collection, Graz
Courtesy Galerie Welz, Salzburg

Klimt spent the summer of 1913 at Lake Garda. The church at Cassone is here depicted from the lake itself, as in some of the views of the Schloss Kammer. Partly due to the hilly terrain, the geometric architectural elements are placed in an orderly arrangement, producing a landscape that is almost cubist in effect. During a visit to Paris in October 1909, Klimt had come into contact with Cubism. Furthermore, he no doubt discussed this new painting phenomenon with Egon Schiele, a member of the League of Austrian Artists, who had also seen an exhibition of Cubist works in Munich in 1912.

Once again it is the overlapping effect of the buildings and cypresses that create the depth to the picture, since there is no diminution in size of any of the elements. Rather than travelling into the distance, the spectator's eye moves up and down the surface of the painting. Paradoxically, for a painter best known for his figurative works, Klimt's landscapes are rarely peopled. Despite the numerous dwellings in the *Church at Cassone*, its atmosphere is of quietness, and the subtitle, *Landscape with Cypresses* is very appropriate. The cypress trees, in symbolic terms, are largely a death and mortuary emblem: cypresses were believed to preserve the body from corruption, hence its use in cemeteries.

94

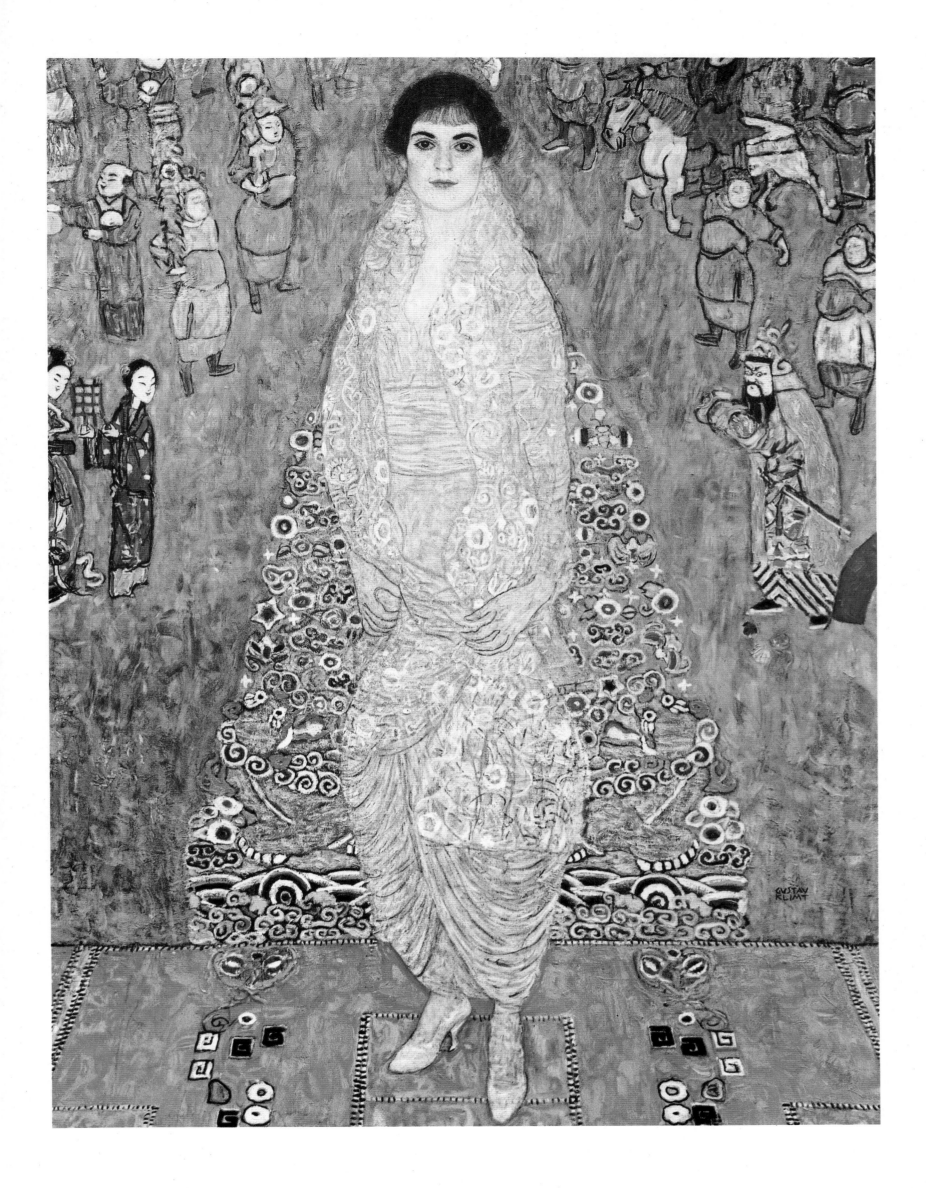

Previous page:

Portrait of Baroness Elisabeth Bachofen-Echt, c. 1914

Oil on canvas
70⅞×50⅜ inches (180×128cm)
Private collection, courtesy Galerie
Welz, Salzburg

After 1910 the pattern of Klimt's life became less varied and he retreated further into isolation since many of his contemporaries in Vienna had left the city or died. Thus, in his work Klimt became increasingly influenced by foreign artists, in particular the French Nabis. In addition to some cross-fertilization of artistic ideas brought about by his contact with Egon Schiele, the major stylistic devices remained those derived from Klimt's collection of eastern art. In a series of portraits, the backgrounds are filled with figures taken from Chinese, Japanese and Korean art.

In the *Portrait of Baroness Elisabeth Bachofen-Echt,* the daughter of August and Serena Lederer, the background is decorated with Chinese-inspired figures. Directly behind the figure of Elisabeth, a floral pattern encloses her body in a triangular structure, a compositional device that links the foreground and the background.

Once again Klimt has retained a naturalistic rendering for Elisabeth's face, but her hands are treated less so. Rather like the Chinese figures behind her, Elisabeth's hands have been defined by a dark outline and their pose contrasts dramatically with the relaxed expression on her face.

Unterach on the Attersee, 1915

Oil on canvas
43⅓×43⅓ inches (110×110cm)
Residenzgalerie, Salzburg

In the landscapes painted in 1915 and 1916, Klimt's interest in representing the structure of an object recedes into the background. In its place is the strong, two dimensionality that characterizes his early works. Furthermore, *Unterach on the Attersee* verges on the monochrome, relieved only by the small areas of red and white in the walls and roofs of the houses.

This starker mood continued to appear in Klimt's work until his death, not only in his landscapes, but in the portraits of *Barbara Flöge* and *Charlotte Pulitzer,* both painted in gray and green tones. No doubt the outbreak of World War I in the fall of 1914 and the death of his mother in 1915 had their effect on Klimt's mood, leading him to do away with any ornament. But in subject matter, the landscapes and portraits never betray any trace of the horrors going on around him. Between 1912 and 1917, Klimt's work remained somewhat static. Only in the work from the last months of his life is another change in style detectable.

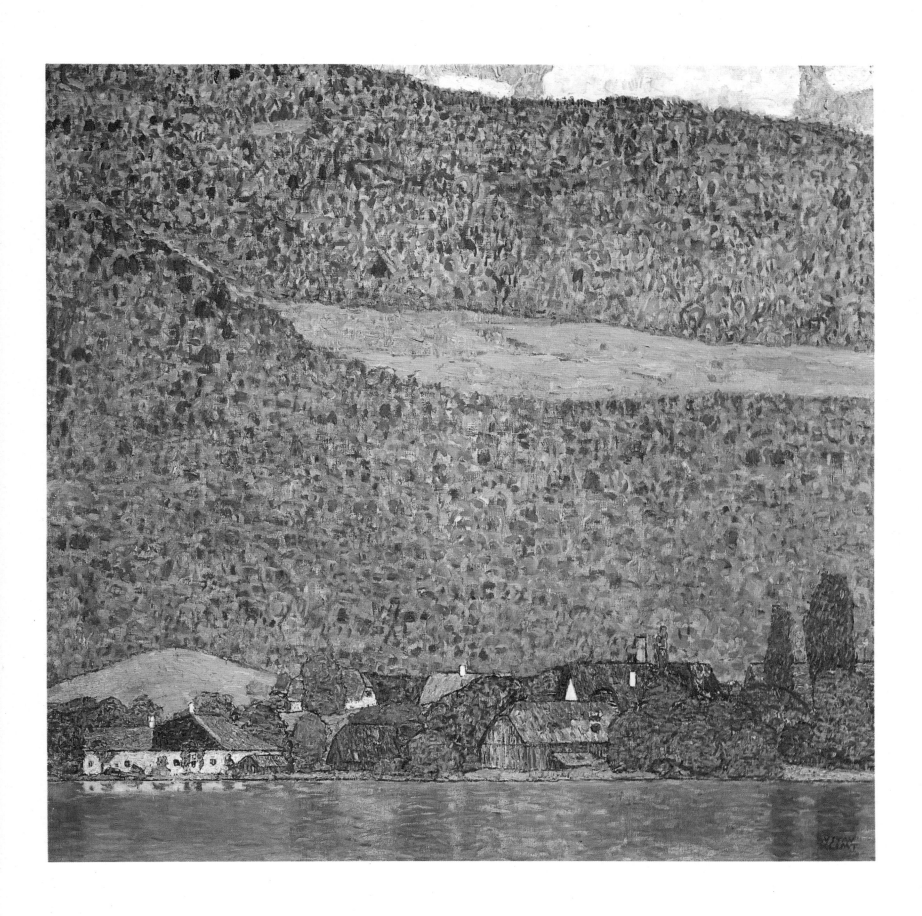

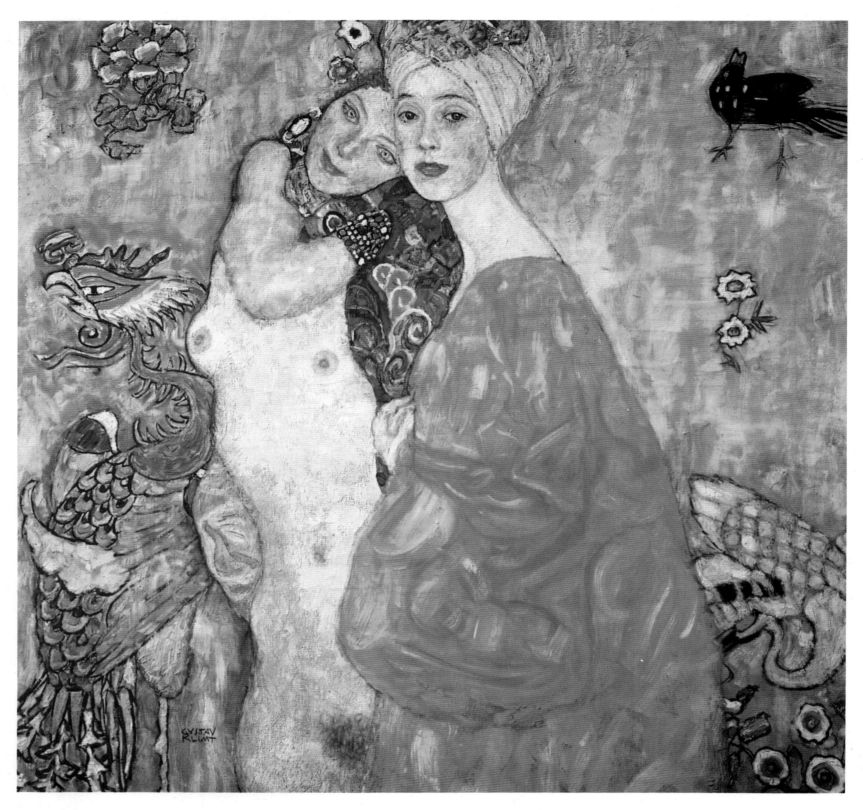

The Friends, 1916-17

Oil on canvas
40×40(?) inches (99×99[?]cm)
Destroyed by fire, 1945

The theme of female friendship and female sexuality was one that Klimt constantly returned to in both his paintings and drawings. In 1915 Klimt temporarily abandoned strong colors in his portraits and produced two works in predominantly gray and green tones: the *Portrait of Barbara Flöge* (the mother of Emilie Flöge) and the *Portrait of Charlotte Pulitzer* (the mother of Serena Lederer).

By 1916, however, Klimt has returned to decorative effects produced not by gold but by line and color. The decorative use of oriental motifs parallels the role that the inlays and mosaics had played in his earlier works and also echoes some of

Van Gogh's paintings that Klimt had seen at the sixteenth Secession exhibition and the large Van Gogh exhibition at the Galerie Miethke in 1907.

Here the background is decorated with fabulous birds and flowers. The figures, placed flat against the background, compress the picture space and remove any idea of an identifiable location.

Portrait of Friederike Maria Beer, 1916

Oil on canvas
66⅛×57⅙ inches (168×130cm)
Private collection, courtesy Galerie Welz, Salzburg

In 1914 Klimt's contemporary Egon Schiele painted the portrait of Friederike Maria Beer, the daughter of a Viennese

nightclub owner. The wealthy young Jewish girl who patronized the Wiener Werkstätte was well known in the artistic circles of Vienna for her friendship with the artist Hans Bohler. All commentators agree that Klimt's portrait of Friederike is the more successful of the two although it is also the more conventional portrait.

Friederike is dressed in a richly decorated jacket and pantaloons. She faces front and is placed against a background of oriental figures. According to Friederike herself, the background was derived from the decoration on a Korean vase in Klimt's extensive collection housed in his studio in the Seldmuhlgasse in Hietzing.

During the late 1960s in order to finance her last years in a retirement home in Hawaii, Friederike Maria Beer sold both the Schiele and Klimt portraits.

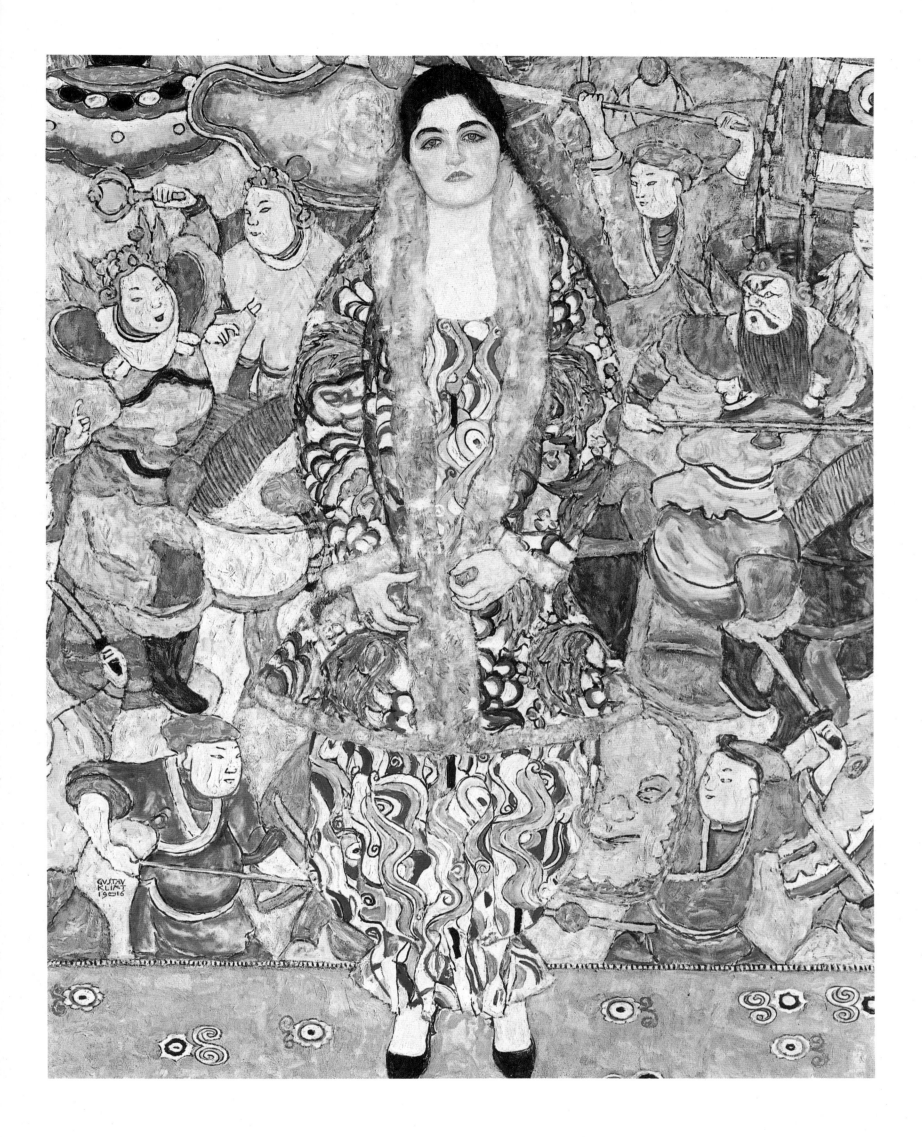

The Dancer, c. 1916-18

Oil on canvas
$70^{7}/_{8} \times 35^{7}/_{16}$ inches (180×90cm)
Private collection, courtesy Galerie St
Etienne, New York

The Dancer began its life as a commissioned portrait of Ria Munk who, like Margaret Stonborough-Wittgenstein had done earlier, eventually refused the portrait. Klimt subsequently reworked the portrait as *The Dancer*.

In spite of what is implied by the title, the female figure is not suggestive of dance or movement: her weight is evenly distributed on both legs in a static pose, her body frontal while her head is turned to the right. In this pose, she is the figure of *Expectation* from the *Stoclet Frieze* in a new painterly style.

What is interesting about this painting is the introduction of the round table at the lower left, of which we see the legs and vase of flowers in elevation and the table top in plan in manner akin to the methods of the Cubist painters. Although we seem to be looking up at the figure of the dancer, we are at the same time looking down at the table top. Again oriental motifs decorate the upper part of the background while the lower section is broken up into areas of geometric patterns and colors. In the left side of the painting with the table, we have a sense of some foreground and background space, while in the right side, the space has been compressed to a point where the figure begins to merge with the background decoration.

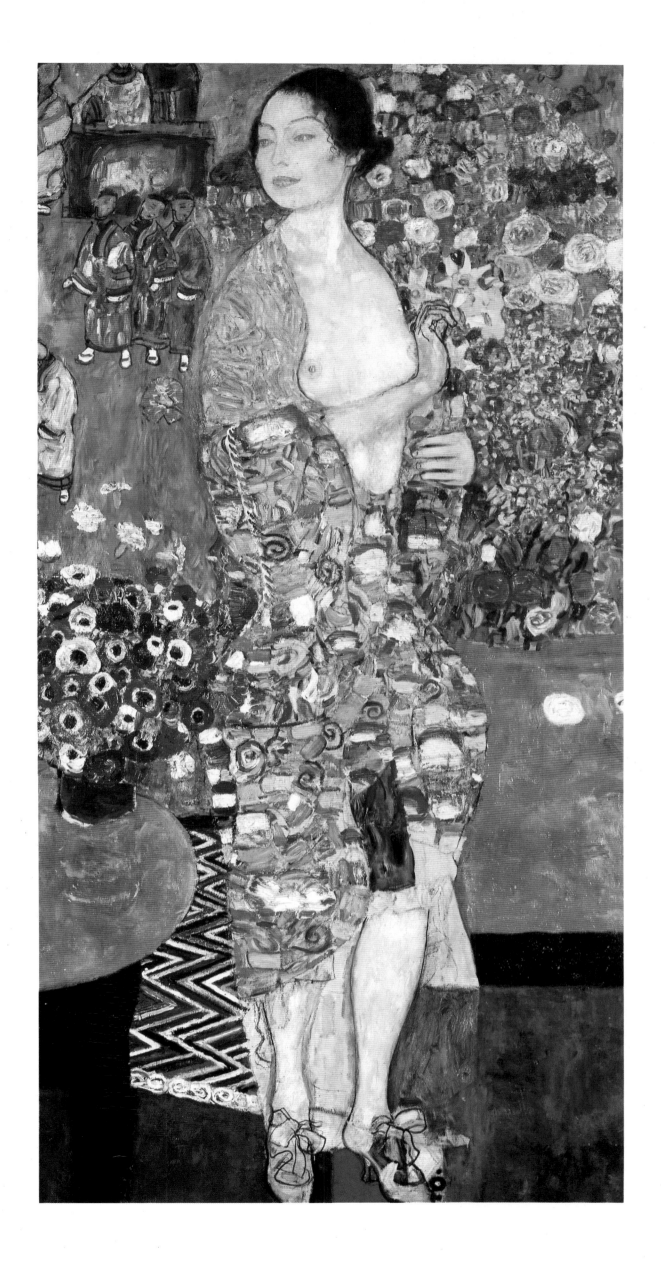

The Bride, 1917-18 (unfinished)
Oil on canvas
$65\frac{3}{8} \times 74\frac{3}{4}$ inches (166×190cm)
Private collection

For five years between 1912 and 1917, Klimt's art appeared as though it could advance no further. Then, in the very last months of his life, from the beginning of 1917 until his death in February of 1918, the beginnings of a new style emerged.

Certain aspects of his earlier style remain in the interest in patterns, decoration, color and line, but there is now an increased concern with the geometric structure of his compositions. This interest in the problems and nature of structure of his works is an indication of the influence that the contact with Egon Schiele was having. There are, however, familiar 'Klimtian' elements: the sleeping central figure with her head turned; the intertwined group of figures and the rear view of the torso at the bottom left are familiar from Klimt's earlier works such as *The Virgin*, *Death and Life* and *Goldfish*. Yet the abstract elements of the composition are favored over the representational and spatial.

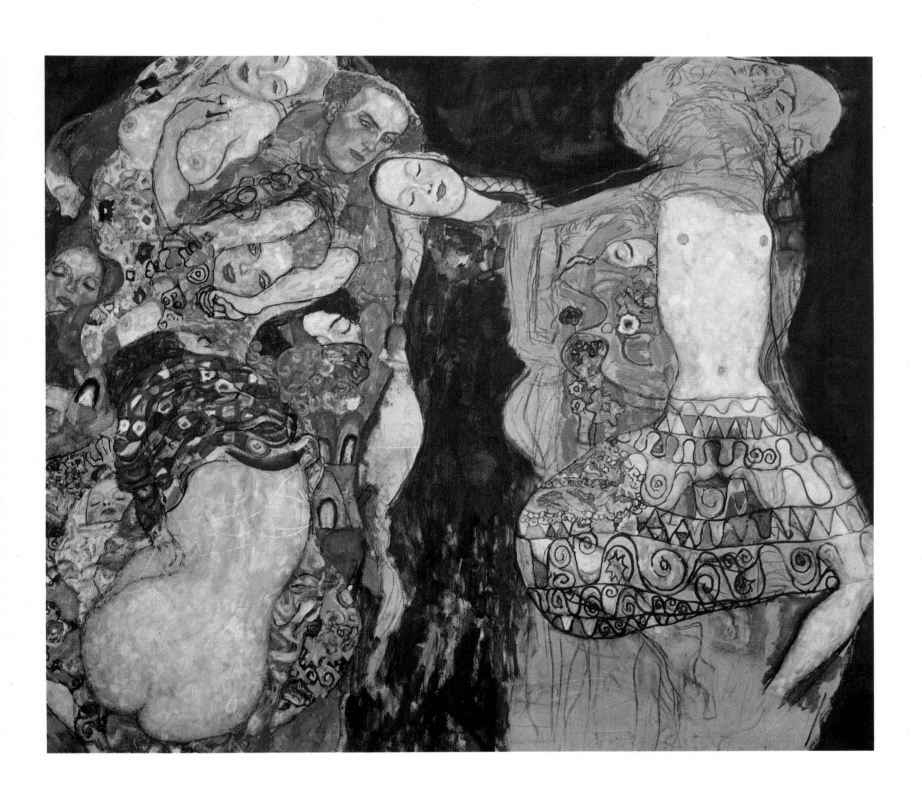

Baby, 1917-18

Oil on canvas
$43\frac{1}{3} \times 43\frac{1}{3}$ inches (110×110cm)
National Gallery of Art, Washington

The receding triangular form of *The Baby* which is the structural basis for this composition is comparable to the paintings produced by Egon Schiele in the years between 1915 and 1916, in particular his *Death and the Maiden* (1915) and *The Embrace* (1915)

In Klimt's new painterly forms, he abandons illusionism completely and the meticulous outlines of his early style. These are replaced by more restrained elements and a new weightlessness.

Baby is only superficially linked with Klimt's earlier representations of childhood such as in *Death and Life, The Three Ages of Woman* (page 63) or even *Philosophy* from the University paintings, for there now remains very little of the traditional allegory.

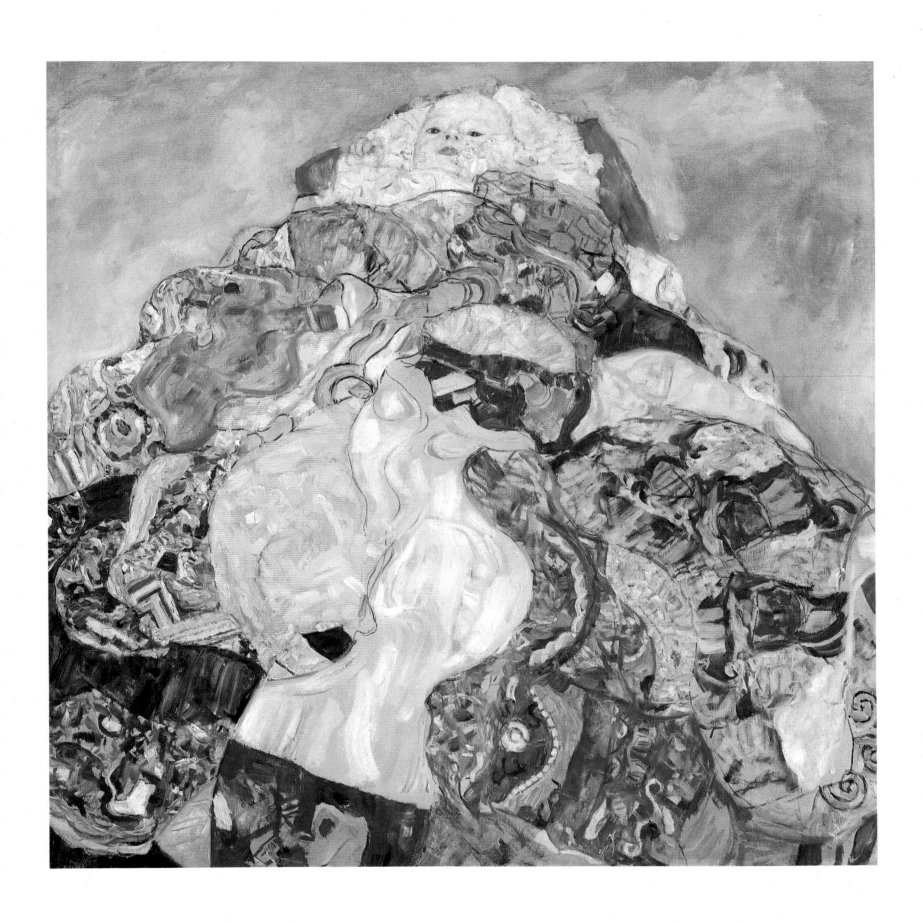

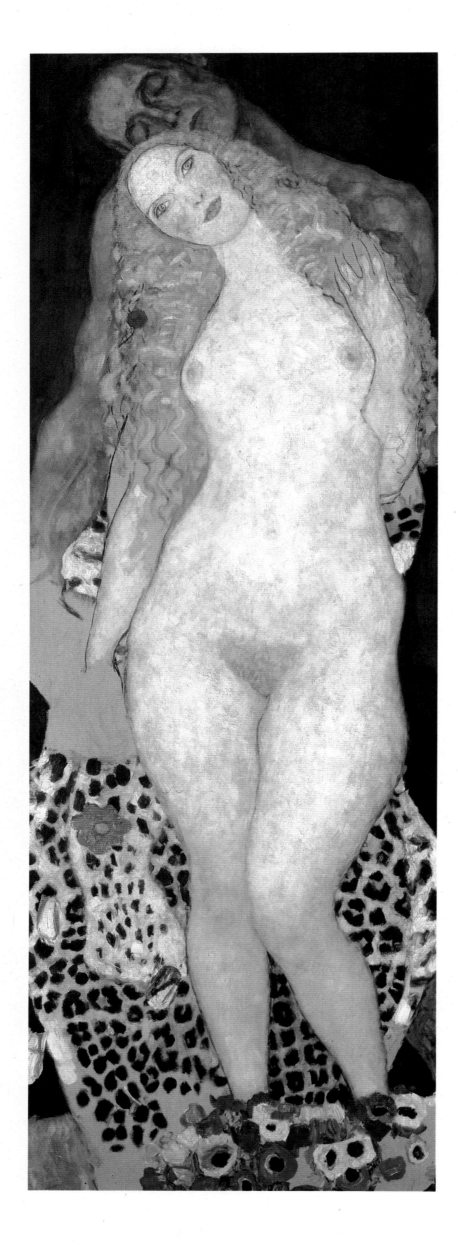

Adam and Eve, 1917-18

Oil on canvas
68⅛×23⅝ inches (173×60cm)
Österreichische Galerie, Vienna

In the early period of Klimt's career, the rare representations of male figures in his allegorical paintings were assigned the dominant roles as the strong redeemer of mankind.

In this painting, the figure of Adam merely exists. In fact, without the title we would not be able to define the two figures in *Adam and Eve* as 'belonging' to each other in any way for there is no gestural communication between them. In addition to excluding any spatial reality, Klimt has also avoided any reference to social or historical realities.

Portrait of Johanna Staude,

1917-18 (unfinished)
Oil on canvas
27½×19¹¹⁄₁₆ inches (70×50cm)
Österreichische Galerie, Vienna

Shortly before his death in February 1918, Klimt returned to the more traditional style of portraits of his early career where half figures are placed against a neutral background. But rather than subdued, the colors are bright and often gaudy.

Johanna Staude is depicted full face in a large leaf-patterned coat with a fur collar against an orange-red background. Unfinished at Klimt's death, it is unlikely that the background has been given its final colors or that Johanna's face has received the final touches.

The new experiments in Klimt's art were cut short by his death and the unfinished canvasses are too incomplete to see what direction his work would have taken.

106

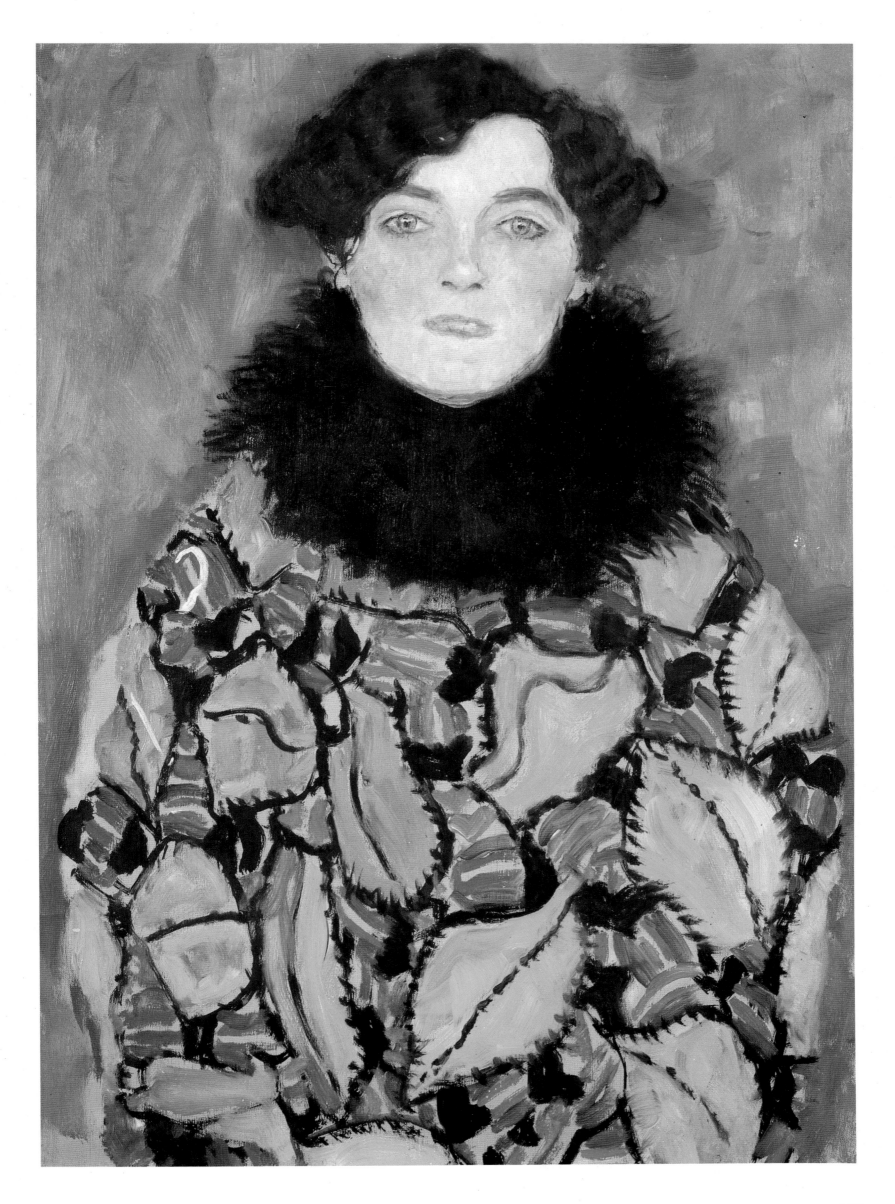

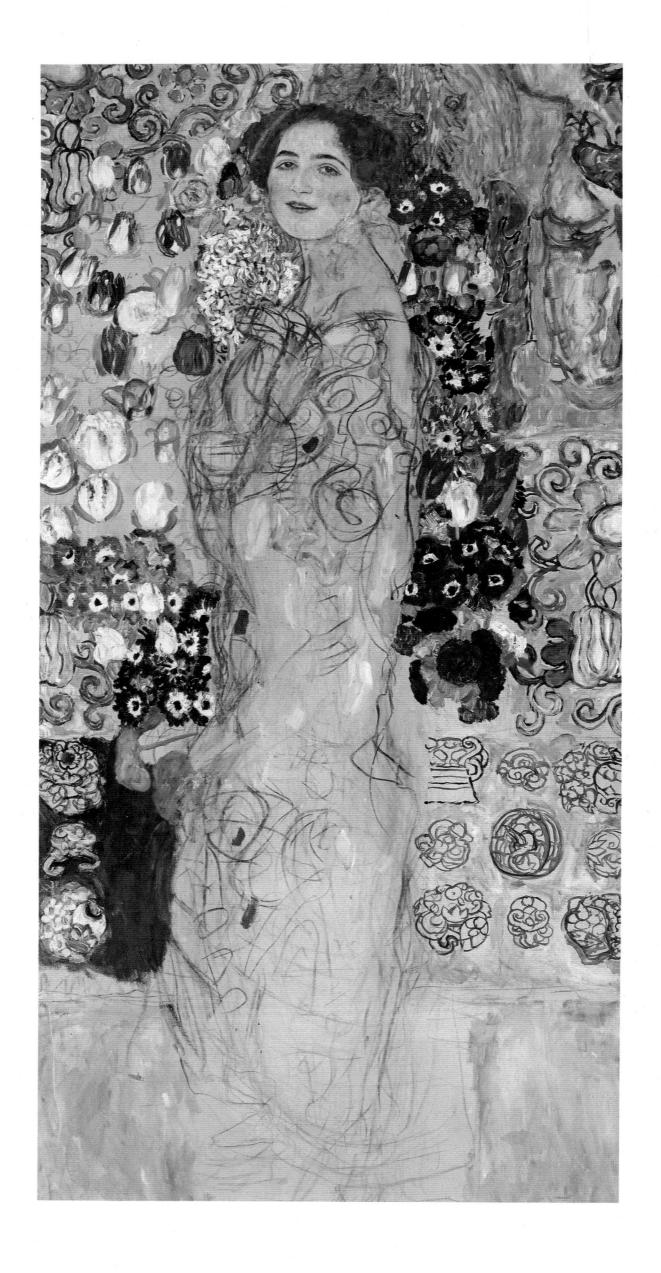

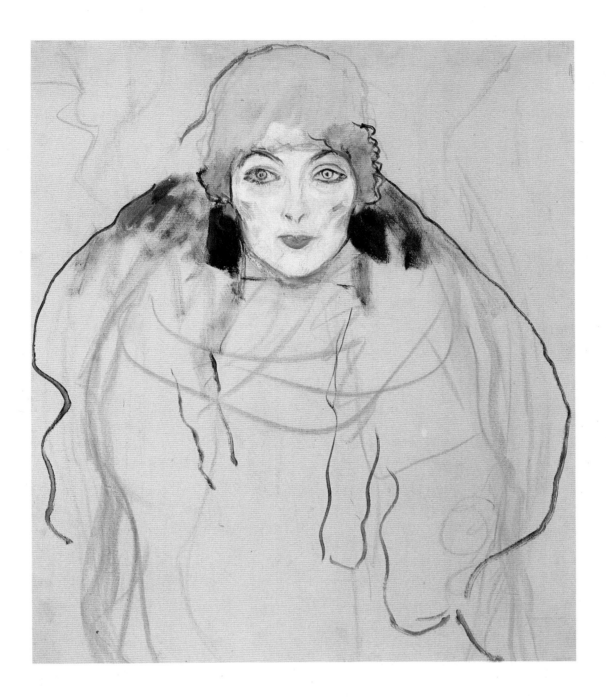

Portrait of a Lady, 1917-18

Oil on canvas
$70^5/_8 \times 35^3/_{16}$ inches (180×90cm)
Neue Galerie der Stadt Linz
Wolfgang-Gurlitt-Museum

Although Klimt's unfinished canvasses leave us in the dark as to the direction his painting was taking, they do, however, provide us with an insight into his working methods.

Having rapidly sketched in the figure, Klimt painted in the features of the model. In *Portrait of a Lady*, we can see how the dabs of color on the unfinished dress – pink, pale blue and a darker blue – are colors that have been picked up from the background scheme. The same colors also occur in the reflected light on the model's face.

Not only is the painting style much looser, the initial drawing shows how far Klimt had moved from the academic conceptions of art in his early career in the carefully drawn and modeled figures to an emphasis on color and pattern in his later years.

Portrait of a Lady, Facing,

1917-18 (unfinished)

Oil on canvas
$26^3/_8 \times 22$ inches (67×56cm)
Neue Galerie der Stadt Linz
Wolfgang-Gurlitt-Museum

The number of unfinished canvasses in Klimt's studio at his death indicates how he was working on a number of paintings simultaneously, something he had done throughout his career.

After Klimt's death, Egon Schiele suggested the idea of preserving Klimt's studio for posterity, but the shortage of accommodation at the end of the war made it necessary to convert the studio into apartments. The breakup of the studio and the distribution of his works consequently led to a number of documents going astray. What insight into Klimt's personality or works these documents would have given us is hard to estimate. Illuminating however, is an undated note that Klimt wrote to himself:

There is no self-portrait of me. I am not interested in myself as material for a picture, rather in other people, especially women. . . . There's nothing remarkable to be seen in me.

Klimt's basic message seems to be that we shouldn't look to him for the meaning but to his works.

Short Bibliography

This is a very select bibliography; for further reading, see Gottfried Fliedl *Gustav Klimt,* Cologne, 1989

Comini, Alessandra *Gustav Klimt,* London, 1975
L'Apocalypse Joyeuse: Vienne 1880-1938 (exhibition catalogue, Centre Georges Pompidou, Paris, 1986)
Dobai, Johannes *Opera Completa di Klimt,* Milan, 1978
Fliedl, Gottfried *Gustav Klimt,* Cologne, 1989
Novotny, Fritz and Dobai, Johannes *Gustav Klimt,* Salzburg,

1967 (catalogue raisonné)
Vergo, Peter 'Gustav Klimt's Beethoven Frieze,' *Burlington Magazine,* CV, (1973), pp 109-113
—— *Art in Vienna, 1898-1918,* Oxford, 1975
Vienna, 1900: Art, Architecture, and Design (exhibition catalogue, Museum of Modern Art, New York, 1986)

Index

Figures in *italics* refer to illustrations; all works of art are by Klimt unless otherwise indicated.

Adam and Eve 106
Allegories and Emblems 7, 10, 22, 23, 30, 34
Altar of Apollo 7
Altar of Dionysus 7
Ancient Egyptian I and II 28-29, 30
Ancient Greek I and II 28-9
Ars 15
Art Nouveau 8, 10
Ashbee, C.R. 14
Association of Visual Artists (Genossenschaft der Bildender Künstler) 8
Attersee 21, 46
Auditorium in the Old Burgtheater, Vienna 24, 25
Austrian Museum for Art and Industry 7
Avenue in the Park of the Schloss Kammer 86, 87

Baby 104, 105
Bahr, Hermann 9, 41
   work by 41
Baroque art 22
Beech Wood I 49, 82
Beer, Friederike Maria 98
Beethoven Frieze 14-15, 16, 18-19, 26, 33, 48, 49, 52, 54-5, 58, 78, 90
Berger, Professor Julius Viktor 7
Berlin 19
   Künstlerhaus 62
Birchwood, The 49
Bloch, Ferdinand 70
Bloch-Bauer, Adèle 8, 70
Böcklin, Arnold 9, 47
Bohler, Hans 98
Bolzano, Vogelweide Memorial 26
Bonnard, Pierre 19
Brahms, Johannes 64
Bride, The 102, 103
Brussels, Palais Stoclet 10, 16, 58
Bucharest, Municipal Theater 7

Byzantine influence 15, 58

Carrière, Eugène 9
Cézanne, Paul 86
Chariot of Thespis 7, 8
Chinese influence 84, 96
Church at Cassone 94
Cottage Garden with Sunflowers 68, 69
Cradle see *Baby*
Crane, Walter 9, 10
Cubism 94, 100

Danae 19, 21, 72, 73, 74, 75
Dancer, The 100, 101
Death and Life 62, 90, 91, 102, 104
Death and the Maiden 104
Debussy, Claude 47
   work by 47
Degas, Edgar 80
   work by 80
Denis, Maurice 19
Dresden, Great Art Exhibition 16
Dumba, Nikolaus 10, 33, 42
Duncan, Isadora 19

Egyptian influence 58, 77
Embrace, The 104
Engelhart, 16
Expectation 58, 59, 100

Fable 22, 23
Fellner, 7
Fiume, Municipal Theater 7
Flaubert, Gustave 19
Flöge, Emilie 8, 21, 48, 64, 88
   Helen 8, 21, 43, 48
Flower Garden 69
Forest of Firs I and II 49
Forstner, Leopold 16, 58
Four Seasons, The 7, 22
Franz Josef, Emperor 8, 24
Freud, Sigmund 19
   work by 19
Friends, The 98
Fulfillment 58, 60
Furstel, Heinrich von 8, 41

Gauguin, Paul 9, 86
Genossenschaft *see* Künstlergenossenschaft
Genossenschaft Bildender Künstler *see* Association of Visual Artists
Gerlach, Martin 7, 10, 22, 23, 30, 33
Gide, André 47
   work by 47
Girl from Tanagra 30
Golden Knight, The 16
Goldfish 16, 47, 102
Guild of Handicrafts 14

Hasenauer, Karl von 7
Helmer, 7
Hevesi, Ludwig 69
Hodler, Ferdinand 13, 15, 49
   work by 12, 15, 49
Hofburg Actor Josef Lewinsky as Carlos 26
Hoffmann, Josef 14, 15, 16, 21, 58, 88
Hope I 19, 50, 62, 74, 90
Hope II 69, 74, 90
Hostile Powers, The 18-19, 52, 54
Hrachowisa, 7
Hygieia (detail from *Medicine*) 13, 41, 44, 45, 58

Idyll 22, 23
Imperial Silver Wedding, masked parade for 7
Impressionism 8, 33, 46
Island in the Attersee 46, 47

Japanese art 10-11, 84, 94
Judith I 52, 53
Judith II (Salome) 19, 75
Jugendstil 10, 15, 30, 36, 72
Jurisprudence 8, 14, 15, 17, 44

Karlsbad, Kurhaus 7
Khnopff, Fernand 9, 36
   work by 9, 36
Kiss, The 15, 18, 58, 62, 68, 69, 78, 79
Klimt, Anna 6
Klimt, Ernst senior 6
Klimt, Ernst junior 7, 8, 26, 30, 43, 48

Klimt, Georg 7, 10, 38
Klimt, Gustav
  allegory 8, 11, 16, 33, 34, 52, 92, 104, 106
  charges of obscenity 11, 13, 19, 41
  childhood 6
  color 14, 21, 96, 98, 100, 102, 106, 108
  color symbolism 92
  decorative materials 8, 14, 16, 18, 33, 44, 47, 52, 58, 66, 80
  decorative symbolism 8, 9, 24, 30, 78, 98, 102
  education 7
  format 24, 36, 38, 46, 74, 77, 84, 86, 88, 100
  geometric forms 15, 48, 84, 88, 102
  Gold Cross of Merit 8, 24
  'golden style' 48, 66, 70, 84
  landscapes 9, 24, 33, 46, 69, 76, 94
  mosaic 58, 66, 70, 78, 98
  Oriental art 11, 21, 84, 100
  patterns 19, 102, 109
  perspective 94, 96, 98
  plein-air painting 21, 77
  studio 7, 8, 98, 109
  technique 8, 41, 42, 46, 66, 100, 106, 109
  textile designs 48
  women 19, 26, 30ff, 41, 51, 72, 75, 80, 81, 98
Klinger, Max 9, 10, 14, 22, 54
  work by 10, 14, 18, 54
Korean art 96, 98

Lady with a Fan 11
Lady with a Feather Hat 80, 81
Lady with a Hat and Feather Boa 80, 81, 84
Lainz, Hermes Villa 7
Landscape with Cypresses see Church at Cassone
Laufberger, Professor Ferdinand 7
League of Austrian Artists 94
Leda 21
Lederer, August 10, 14, 43, 44, 54, 96
Lenz, Max 15
Leonardo da Vinci
  work by 78
lesbian love 51
London, Royal College of Art 7
  South Kensington, Schools of Art 7
Love 19, 30, 31, 50, 58, 78

Mackintosh, Charles and Margaret 14
MacNair, J. H. 14
Mahler, Gustav 64, 76
Makart, Hans 7, 8, 24, 30
  work by 8
Manet, Edouard 9
Matisse, Henri 21
Matsch, Franz 7, 8, 26, 30, 41
  work by 8, 41
Medicine 8, 11, 13, 14, 16, 40, 41, 44, 47, 58
Michelangelo Buonarroti 23
Minnegercde, 7
Moll, Carl 8, 16
Monet, Claude 76
Morris, William 23
Moser, Ditha 44
Moser, Kolo 14, 16

Mucha, Alphonse 9
Munich 8, 16, 38, 94
  Neue Pinakothek 64
Munk, Ria 100
Munkascy, Michael 30
Music (lithograph) 33
Music I 2-3, 15, 26, 32, 33, 54
Music II 14, 15, 33
Mycenaean art 58, 70, 92

Nabis, the 19, 21, 86, 96
Nazarenes, the 30
Neo-Impressionism 21, 82
Nuda Veritas 10, 41
nudity 10, 13, 21, 38, 51
Nur Maler (Pure Painters) 16

Olbrich, Joseph Maria 9-10, 13, 69
On the Attersee I and II 46, 47

Palais Dumba 42
Palais Sturany 7
Pallas Athene 10, 15, 36, 38, 39, 42, 52
Paris, Exposition Universelle 13
Park, The 82, 83
Pelesch, royal palace at 7
Pembauer, Josef 26
Philosophy 8, 10, 11, 13, 15, 41, 43, 44, 104
Poetry 15, 33, 54
Pointillism 46, 82
Portrait of Adèle Bloch-Bauer I 11, 15, 16, 36, 70, 71
Portrait of Adèle Bloch-Bauer II 15, 84, 85
Portrait of a Lady 108, 109
Portrait of a Lady, Facing 109
Portrait of a Lady (Frau Heymann?) 30
Portrait of Barbara Flöge 21, 96, 98
Portrait of Baroness Elisabeth Bachofen-Echt 11, 95, 96
Portrait of Charlotte Pulitzer 21, 96, 98
Portrait of Emilie Flöge 15, 18, 48, 58, 64
Portrait of Eugenia Primavesi 21
Portrait of Friederike Maria Beer 11, 98, 99
Portrait of Fritza Riedler 15, 16, 36, 66, 67, 69, 70
Portrait of Johanna Staude 106, 107
Portrait of Mäda Primavesi 21, 88, 89
Portrait of Margaret Stonborough-Wittgenstein 16, 18, 64, 65, 66
Portrait of Serena Lederer 10, 43, 44
Portrait of Sonja Knips 10, 15, 18, 30, 36, 37, 44, 48, 64, 66, 81
Portrait of the Pianist and Piano Teacher Joseph Pembauer 1, 26, 27
Post-Impressionism 21, 41, 86
Prague, National Gallery 76
Pre-Raphaelite Brotherhood 34
Primavesi, Otto and family 21, 88
Procession of the Dead 16, 18, 62
Puvis de Chavannes, Pierre 9

Ravenna, Church of San Vitale 15, 58, 86
realism 9
Reichenberg (Liberec) 7
Reiner, Georg 26
Renaissance art 7, 22
Rieser, 7

Rococo art 22
Rodin, Auguste 9
  work by 13
Roller, 14
  work by 14
Romanticism 30
Rysselberghe, Theo Van 10

St Louis World Fair 15
Salome see Judith II
Schiele, Egon 16, 19, 21, 94, 96, 102, 104, 109
  work by 21
Schiller, Heinrich 19, 41, 54
  work by 54
Schloss Immendorf 14, 44
Schloss Kammer 21, 94
Schloss Kammer on the Attersee I 76
Schloss Kammer on the Attersee II 76
Schloss Kammer on the Attersee III 77
Schloss on the Water see Schloss Kammer on the Attersee I
Schnitzler, Arthur 26, 30
  work by 30
Schubert at the Piano 10, 13, 14, 15, 26, 33, 41, 42
Sculpture 10
Secession 6, 8-11, 13, 14, 15, 20, 33, 36, 38, 41, 54, 58, 64, 68, 69, 84
  posters for exhibition 12, 36, 38
Segantini, Giuseppe 9
Seurat, Georges 82
Sfumato 14, 41
Shakespeare's Theater 7
Stoclet, Adolphe 16, 58
Stoclet Frieze 10, 15, 16, 18, 19, 20, 59, 66, 78, 80, 86, 92, 100
Stohr, Ernst 44
Stonborough-Wittgenstein, Margaret 8, 64
Stuck, Franz von 9, 10, 22, 38
Sufferings of Weak Humanity, The 54
Sunflower, The 69
Swamp, The 47
Symbolism 8, 11, 19, 34, 47, 68

Theater in Taormina 7, 8
Three Ages of Woman, The 13, 62, 63, 90, 104
Titian 7
Toorop, Jan 14, 16
Tragedy 34, 35
Tree of Life 58, 61

Unterach on the Attersee 96, 97

Van Gogh, Vincent 9, 21, 69, 86
  work by 69, 86
Velázquez, Diego Rodriguez de Silva y 13, 16, 66
  work by 12
Ver Sacrum magazine 19, 33, 36, 41, 44
Vienna 6, 7, 21
  Academy of Fine Arts 6, 7, 8, 13
  Burgtheater 7, 24, 30
  Historisches Museum 64
  Krautkappel 10, 13
  Kunstgewerbeschule 7
  Kunsthistorisches Museum 7, 8, 10, 16,

30, 38, 66
 Künstlerhausgenossenschaft 6-7, 8-9
 Kunstschau 16, 19, 50, 68, 69
 Österreichisches Museum 44
 State Gallery of Modern Art 14
 University, Great Hall 8, 10, 11, 14, 24, 30, 41, 43, 44, 90, 104
Virgin, The 92, *93,* 102
Vlaminck, Maurice de 19

Vuillard, Edouard 19

Wagner, Otto 16
Wärndorfer, Fritz 19, 21, 50, 88
Water Snakes (Friends I) 51
Well-Armed Strong One, The 54
Whistler, James McNeill 9
Wiener Werkstätte 16, 19, 21, 43, 48, 50, 58, 88, 98

Wittgenstein, Karl 64
 Margaret *see* Stonborough-Wittgenstein, Margaret

Yearning for Happiness Finds Fulfillment in Poetry 56
Youth 22

Zola, Emile 19

Acknowledgments

The author would like to thank Veronica Delaney for invaluable assistance with manuscript preparation. The publisher would like to thank Mike Rose, who designed this book, Aileen Reid who edited it, and Moira Dykes, the picture researcher. We would also like to thank the following individuals and institutions for supplying the illustrations:

Archiv für Kunst und Geschichte, Berlin: pages 6, 20 top
Barry Friedman Ltd, New York: page 12 right
Bayerische Staatsgemäldesammlungen (Neue Pinakothek), Munich/PHOTO ARTOTHEK: pages 2-3, 32-33, 65
Bild-Archiv der Österreichischen Nationalbibliothek, Vienna: pages 9 below, 15 right, 16, 17, 18 both, 20 below, 41
Bundesdenkmalamt, Vienna: page 9 top
Historisches Museum der Stadt Wien, Vienna: pages 7, 10 both, 11 top, 12 left, 13 top, 15 left, 19 below, 23, 25, 35, 48 /PHOTOBUSINESS pages 22, 28-29, 30, 31, 39
Kunstmuseum, Bern: page 12 top
The Metropolitan Museum of Art, New York: Purchase Catharine Lorillard Wolfe Collection, Bequest of Catharine Lorillard Wolfe, by exchange, and Wolfe Fund and Gift of Henry Walters, Bequest of Collis P Huntington Munsey and Rogers Funds, by exchange, 1980 (1980.412), page 43 / Gift of Andre and Clara Mertens, in memory of her mother, Jenny Pulitzer Steiner, 1964 (64.148) page 89
Musei Civici Veneziani d'Arte e di Storia/SCALA: page 75

Museum der Bildenden Kunste zu Leipzig: page 19 top
Collection, The Museum of Modern Art, New York: Mr and Mrs Ronald S Lander and Helen Acheson Funds, and Serge Sabarsky: page 74 / Gertrud A Mellon Fund: page 83
National Gallery, Prague: pages 76, 93
National Gallery of Art, Washington: Gift of Otto and Franziska Kallir with the help of the Carol and Edwin Gaines Fullinwider Fund: page 105
National Gallery of Canada, Ottawa: page 50
Neue Galerie der Stadt Linz/Wolfgang-Gurlitt-Museum: pages 108, 109
Österreichische Galerie, Vienna: page 8 /FOTOSTUDIO OTTO pages 37, 51, 53, 54-55 both, 56-57 both, 67, 68, 71, 77, 80, 85, 87, 98, 106, 107 /PHOTOBUSINESS page 79
Österreichischen Museum für Angewandte Kunst/ PHOTOBUSINESS: pages 59, 60, 61
Phaidon Picture Archive: page 14 both
Private Collection, Courtesy Galerie St Etienne, New York: pages 46, 101
Private Collection/PHOTOBUSINESS: pages 73, 81, 91
Rijksmuseum Kröller-Müller, Otterlo: page 11 below
Salzburger Landessammlungen Rupertinum: page 97
Staatliche Kunstsammlung, Dresden/Photo Gerhard Reinhold, Leipzig-Molkau: page 49
Tiroler Landesmuseum, Innsbruck: pages 1, 27
Witt Library, Courtauld Institute of Art, London/ WEIDENFELD ARCHIVE: page 21